ALABAMA

DAILY DEVOTIONS FOR DIE-HARD FANS

CRIMSON TIDE

Daily Devotions for Die-Hard Fans: Alabama Crimson Tide
© 2010, 2013 Ed McMinn
Extra Point Publishers; P.O. Box 871; Perry, GA 31069

Library of Congress Cataloging-in-Publication Data
13 ISBN Digit ISBN: 978-0-9840847-3-9

Manufactured in the United States of America.

Visit us at www.die-hardfans.com for information about other titles in the series.

Cover and interior design by Slynn McMinn.

Every effort has been made to identify copyright holders. Any omissions are unintentional. Extra Point Publishers should be notified in writing immediately for full acknowledgement in future editions.

CRIMSON TIDE

To
the Rev. Don Caulley,
from whom, like the Lord he serves,
flows a vast and gracious Tide

The following titles are available:

DAY 1

GOOD OLD DAYS

Read Psalm 102.

"My days vanish like smoke; . . . but you remain the same,
and your years will never end" (vv. 3, 27).

When we talk about the "good old days," we're probably not thinking about the early days of Alabama football.

Not that the Tide didn't win. Alabama's first-ever football game was on Nov. 11, 1892, against a squad from Birmingham High School. Bama won 56-0 and has never looked back.

The problem was the game itself in those good old days. The whole situation was haphazard, to say the least. For instance, finding a coach who knew anything about the game was difficult. Nine men coached the first fourteen years of Alabama football.

The eligibility rules were rather vague back then. Walter Shafer had been a star fullback at Auburn for four years, and when he enrolled at Alabama in 1896 to study law, he promptly went out for the football team.

The game was also downright brutal in those early days. Thomas Wert, who played for Bama in the late 1890s declared, "In those days, football wasn't a lady's game." He recalled that in one game against Ole Miss in Jackson, when one of their players "tried to move the ball after it was dead, I fell on his neck with my knee." The home crowd didn't appreciate that one bit and promptly emptied out of the grandstands and attacked Wert "with umbrellas, walking canes and the like."

CRIMSON TIDE

When Bama played the Southern Athletic Club in 1899, they had prizefighters and dockhands on their team, according to Wert. "They kicked me, trampled on me, and sometimes bit me all at the same time," Wert said. When the game was over, he had two black eyes, a nose bigger than his fist, and a bad limp.

It was "an irregular game" in those good old days, one we wouldn't recognize today, but no one could doubt that both students and fans adored it.

It's a brutal truth that time just never stands still. The current of your life sweeps you along until you realize one day you've lived long enough to have a past. Part of it you cling to fondly. The stunts you pulled with your high-school buddies. Your first apartment. That dance with your first love. That special vacation. Those "good old days."

You hold on relentlessly to the memory of those old, familiar ways because of the stability they provide in our uncertain world. They will always be there even as times change for the worse and you age -- also for the worse.

Another constant exists in your life too. God has been a part of every event in your life that created a memory because he was there. He's always there with you; the question is whether you ignore him or make him a part of your day.

A "good old day" is any day shared with God.

Older people who forget that they were once boys say that football is a brutal game and that the foolish infatuation will soon die out.
-- 1896 Alabama Yearbook

**Today is one of the "good old days"
if you share it with God.**

ALABAMA

DAY 2

DYNASTY

Read 2 Samuel 7:8-17.

"Your house and your kingdom will endure forever before me; your throne will be established forever" (v. 16).

After Alabama's dismantling of Notre Dame in the 2013 BCS National Championship, the word that had been whispered before the game could be shouted for everyone to hear: "Dynasty!"

ESPN's Gene Wojciechowski made the official pronouncement after Alabama's 42-14 humiliation of the Irish. "We can pretty much hold a retirement party for the 'Is Alabama a Dynasty?' debate," he declared.

The dynasty tag wasn't stuck onto the Tide merely because the win over Notre Dame cemented Alabama's second straight national championship and third in four seasons. As much as anything, it was the way the Tide won this third title. They were perfect, so good that Wojciechowski gushed, "Bama should get a crystal trophy and a half for this one."

Once upon a time, establishing a dynasty in college football was somewhat easier. The wealthier programs simply stockpiled athletes by handing out as many scholarships as they could afford. You got the best athletes while other schools didn't.

Also, in the days before the BCS, the national title contenders didn't necessarily play each other in a bowl game. Witness, for example, Brigham Young's 1984 championship, clinched with a 24-17 win over a five-loss Michigan team in the Holiday Bowl.

Thus, what Alabama has done in this modern age is, to quote Wojciechowski again, "beyond impressive; it's historic." It's also dynastic, though head coach Nick Saban would have none of it. "I don't think words like 'dynasty' are really words I'm interested in," he said. What he is interested in, he said, is accomplishment.

Nevertheless, even if Saban wouldn't admit to it, that accomplishment created a dynasty in Tuscaloosa.

Inevitably, someone will knock Alabama from its lofty perch. History teaches us that kingdoms, empires, countries, and even sports programs rise and fall. Dynasties end as events and circumstances conspire and align to snap all winning streaks.

Your life is like that; you win some and you lose some. You get a promotion on Monday and your son gets arrested on Friday. You breeze through your annual physical but your dog dies. You finally line up a date with that cutie next door and get sent out of town on business.

Only one dynasty will never end because it is based upon an everlasting promise from God. God promised David the king an enduring line in the appearance of one who would establish God's kingdom forever. That one is Jesus Christ, the reigning king of God's eternal and unending dynasty.

The only way to lose out on that one is to stand on the sidelines and not get in the game.

Dynasty. I say it all day. Unprecedented. Dynasty, man!
-- Alabama long snapper Carson Tinker

All dynasties and win streaks end except the one
God established with Jesus as its king;
this one never loses and never will.

DAY 3

WEATHERPROOFED

Read Nahum 1:3-9.

"His way is in the whirlwind and the storm, and clouds are the dust of his feet" (v. 3b).

It became known as "The Shot That Saved Lives."

On March 14, 2008, Alabama met Mississippi State in the second round of the SEC Tournament in the Georgia Dome. The season had not been a kind one for the Tide, but they upset defending national champion Florida in the opening round and then fought the top seed in the SEC West down to the last shot.

State led 59-56 with two seconds left, but Bama had the ball after a timeout. Everyone in the Dome knew that senior Tide guard Mykal Riley would get the ball. Riley was "not a superstar, not even truly a scorer, because he rarely drives to the hoop. Mykal is a shooter." And right now Alabama needed a shot.

In the huddle, Tide coach Mark Gottfried told Riley to run off a screen, grab the inbounds pass, and fire away. Exhausted, Riley prayed, "Lord, please let me hit this shot." Alabama forward Demetrius Jemison got the ball to Riley on the left wing. State tried to foul, knowing that two free throws would do no harm, but no foul was called.

Riley let fly. The ball was airborne when time expired and the horn blared. The shot fell through the net. Overtime.

About eight minutes later, with 2:11 left in overtime, the crowd in the Dome heard a disquieting roaring sound. The roof rippled, insulation floated downward, and metal washers fell onto the court. A tornado with winds of 120 mph had passed just north of the Dome. It flipped cars over, toppled light towers, and collapsed a brick wall onto a homeless man, killing him.

But all 14,825 folks in the Dome were safe. No one was even injured -- because they were watching the overtime forced by Mykal Riley's shot. If he had missed, several thousand persons would have left the building, many of them walking to their hotels. They would have been right in the path of the storm.

A thunderstorm washes away your golf game or the picnic with the kids. Lightning knocks out the electricity just as you settle in at the computer. A tornado interrupts your Sunday dinner and sends everyone scurrying to the hallway. A hurricane cancels your beach trip.

For all our technology and all our knowledge, we are still at the mercy of the weather, able only to get a little more advance warning than in the past. It isn't enough as the tragedy of the tornadoes all too clearly illustrates. The weather answers only to God. Rain and hail will fall where they want to.

We stand mute before the awesome power of the weather, but we should be even more awestruck at the power of the one who controls it, a power beyond our imagining. Neither, however, can we imagine the depths of God's love for us, a love that drove him to die on a cross for us.

This was a walking crowd.
-- Georgia Dome spokeswoman Ashley Boatman

**Almighty God's power is beyond anything
we can imagine, but so is his love for us.**

DAY 4

SMART MOVE

Read 1 Kings 4:29-34; 11:1-6.

"[Solomon] was wiser than any other man. . . . As Solomon grew old, his wives turned his heart after other gods, and his heart was not fully devoted to the Lord his God" (vv. 4:31, 11:4).

What in the world was Alabama softball coach Patrick Murphy thinking?

A loss to Michigan put the collective backs of the 52-10 Tide up against the wall in the 2009 Women's College World Series. They responded by slamming eight-time NCAA champion Arizona 14-0 in an elimination game. That marked the most lopsided win in the 27-year history of the World Series and broke a 20-year series record for runs scored in a game.

But that only set up a sudden-death date with Arizona State, the defending national champs, and that game was anything but a blowout. A two-run homer in the top of the fourth propelled the Wildcats to a 2-0 lead.

The Tide launched a rally in the bottom of the inning by loading the bases with two outs. That brought senior speedster Brittany Rogers to the plate. Rogers is one of the greatest players in Bama softball history. She was a four-time All-America, set the school record for career stolen bases, and had the second-highest career batting average (.417) in Alabama history. She was exactly the player the Tide needed in that pressure-packed situation.

That's when Murphy "tossed the biggest curveball of the tournament." He called for a pinch hitter. Not just any pinch hitter, but a freshman who hadn't batted in two weeks and who hadn't had a base hit in 38 days.

So how did Jazlyn Lunceford respond? She unloaded with a grand slam, and the Tide never looked back, winning 6-2.

Smart move, coach.

Remember that time on your way to work you wrecked the car when you spilled hot coffee in your lap? That cold morning you fell out of the boat? The time you gave your honey a tool box for her birthday?

Formal education notwithstanding, we all make some dumb moves sometime because time spent in a classroom is not an accurate gauge of common sense. Folks impressed with their own smarts often grace us with erudite pronouncements that we intuitively recognize as flawed, unworkable, or simply wrong.

A good example is the observation that great intelligence and scholarship are not compatible with faith in God. That is, the more we come to know, the less we are able to believe. But any incompatibility occurs only because we begin to trust in our own wisdom rather than the wisdom of God. We forget, as Solomon did, that God is the ultimate source of all our knowledge and wisdom and that even our ability to learn is a gift from God.

Not smart at all.

I just felt good about her. I just had, I guess, a gut feeling.
-- Tide coach Patrick Murphy on his decision to bat Jazlyn Lunceford

**Being truly smart means trusting in God's
wisdom rather than only in our own knowledge.**

DAY 5

UNEXPECTEDLY

Read Luke 2:1-20.

"She gave birth to her firstborn, a son. She wrapped him in cloths and placed him in a manger, because there was no room for them in the inn" (v. 7).

The Texas Longhorns did something unexpected, but so did the Tide, and the result all but clinched the national championship.

On Jan. 7, 2010, in the Rose Bowl, Texas took an early 6-0 lead in the BCS National Championship Game. The rest of the first half, though, belonged to Alabama. On the last play of the first quarter, a nine-yard run by Heisman-Trophy winner Mark Ingram placed the ball at the Longhorn three. Two plays later, he took advantage of a block from Terrence Cody to step untouched into the end zone. Alabama led 7-6.

With 8:44 to go in the half, Trent Richardson broke a 49-yard run for a 14-6 lead. After a Javier Arenas interception and a subsequent defensive stand and punt return, Leigh Tiffin nailed a field goal. Alabama led 17-6 with only 29 seconds to go in the half.

With their star quarterback, Colt McCoy, on the sidelines and everything about the game going Alabama's way, the logical move for Texas seemed to be to take a knee and flee to the locker room at halftime to regroup. That certainly appeared to be what the Horns were doing with a conservative, first-down run. The run gained nine yards to the 37, and Texas called time out.

Then came the unexpected play that "will be debated by

CRIMSON TIDE

Longhorn nation for years to come." Hoping to catch the Tide defense by surprise, Texas tried a shovel pass. But sophomore lineman Marcell Dareus -- the game's defensive MVP -- tipped the ball and then caught it. He stiffarmed the Texas quarterback to the ground and rumbled 28 yards for a touchdown.

Unexpectedly, Bama led 24-6. The national championship was suddenly pretty much in the bag. Alabama, of course, won 37-21.

Just like the Texas Longhorns, we think we've got everything figured out and planned for, and then something unexpected happens, like a great play from a star lineman. Someone gets ill; you fall in love; you lose your job; you're going to have another child. Life surprises us with its bizarre twists and turns.

God is that way too, catching us unawares to remind us he's still around. A friend who hears you're down and stops by, a child's laugh, an achingly beautiful sunset -- unexpected moments of love and beauty. God is like that, always doing something in our lives we didn't expect.

But why shouldn't he? There is nothing God can't do. The only factor limiting what God can do is the paucity of our own faith.

We should expect the unexpected from God, this same deity who unexpectedly came to live among us as a man. He does, by the way, expect a response from you.

I can't believe I pulled off that screen. I could not wait to get into the end zone.
> *– Marcell Dareus on his interception and touchdown*

**God does the unexpected – like showing up
as Jesus -- to remind you of his presence,
and now he expects a response from you.**

FAIL-SAFE

Read Luke 22:54-62.

"Peter remembered the word the Lord had spoken to him: 'Before the rooster crows today, you will disown me three times.' And he went outside and wept bitterly" (vv. 61b-62).

Wallace Wade's early success at Alabama set him up for inevitable failure.

Wade was 31 when he arrived in Tuscaloosa in 1923 to take over the Tide football program. He went 15-3-1 his first two seasons. Then in 1925, he made history when the undefeated Tide became the first Southern team to play in the Rose Bowl.

All-American quarterback Pooley Hubert scored one touchdown and hit halfback Johnny Mack Brown – "Alabama's first true national football star" – with a pair of scoring tosses to pace the Tide to a 20-19 win. The outcome "shocked West Coast fans and reporters" and gave Alabama its first national title. The 1926 squad was also undefeated, made another trip to Pasadena, and tied Stanford 7-7.

The Tide thus went into the 1927 season having ripped off 22 straight regular-season wins. When the team went 5-4-1, though, the grumbling began; it only increased when the 1928 and '29 squads both went 6-3. The truth became obvious: "By having such unparalleled success early on, Wade had created his own impossible act to follow." He obviously heard the mounting criticism and was affected by it. At the end of the 1929 season, he announced that he had accepted the head coaching job at Duke, but that he would not start there until 1931. He had a contract to complete the 1930 season at Alabama and would honor it.

The 1930 team may have been Wade's best. The Tide went 10-0, crushed Washington State 24-0 in the Rose Bowl, and won another national title. After the season, though, his head held high, he moved on.

Failure is usually defined by expectations. Wallace Wade's career at Alabama was certainly not a failure, though his team's perceived failings led him to leave. A baseball player who hits .300 is a star, but he fails seventy percent of the time. We grumble about a postal system that manages to deliver billions of items without a hitch.

And we are often our own harshest critics, beating ourselves up for our failings because we expected better. Never mind that our expectations were unrealistic to begin with.

The bad news about life is that failure – unlike success -- is inevitable. Only one man walked this earth perfectly and we're not him. The good news about life, however, is that failure isn't permanent. In life, we always have time to reverse our failures as did Peter, he who failed our Lord so abjectly.

The same cannot be said of death. In death we eternally suffer the consequences of our failure to follow that one perfect man.

The best you can do is not good enough unless it does the job.
-- Wallace Wade

Only one failure in life dooms us to eternal failure in death: failing to follow Jesus Christ.

DAY 7

IN LOSS, VICTORY

Read John 11:17-44.

"Jesus said to them, 'Take off the grave clothes and let him go'" (v. 44b).

The greatest victory of his life came after Jermareo Davidson suffered the greatest loss of his life.

From 2003-'07, Davidson was a power forward during one of the greatest runs in Bama basketball history. It included three trips to the NCAA Tournament (including one to the Elite Eight) and three 20-win seasons.

In November 2006, his senior season, Davidson received a call from a family friend with the awful news that his older brother had been shot and was in an Atlanta hospital. Davidson called Nikki Murphy, his girlfriend, and together they visited his brother, who was paralyzed and on a ventilator.

After Davidson played in the Tide's season-opening win over Jackson State, Nikki and he drove back to Atlanta. On the trip home, Nikki swerved to avoid another vehicle and lost control of her Explorer. Davidson walked away unharmed, but Nikki was thrown free. She died several hours later in the same hospital where on Dec. 20, Davidson's brother died.

He found valuable therapy in basketball, returning to the team after missing only one game. "I don't know if I'd be strong enough even to think about basketball," teammate Ronald Steele said.

How did Davidson find the strength? The answer lay in the

surprise announcement he made to his mother the night before his brother's funeral: He wanted to be baptized during the funeral in the church his brother and he had attended as children. After the eulogy, the pastor asked if anyone wanted to be saved, and Davidson stepped forward. "In a church that was filled to capacity, a grieving giant kneeled on a pillow, asked for forgiveness and gave his life to the Lord."

And achieved his greatest victory.

We all have times of defeat and loss in our lives, but nothing fills us with such an overwhelming sense of helplessness as the death of a loved one. There's absolutely nothing we can do about it. Like Jermareo Davison with the double tragedy in his life, we, too, can only stand helpless and weep as something precious and beautiful leaves us.

For the believer in Jesus Christ and his loved ones, though -- like Mary and Martha and Jermareo Davidson -- resurrection and life follow burial and death. Faith in Jesus transforms loss into victory, not only for the loved one but for those left behind. Amid our tears and our sense of loss, we celebrate the ultimate victory of our family member or friend. Amid death, we find life; amid sorrow, we find hope.

Through Jesus, we snatch victory from the jaws of defeat.

Nobody could tell whether it was holy water or tears running down Jermareo Davidson's face.

— Sportswriter Grant Wahl

**Faith in Jesus means our tears at a funeral
are for ourselves and the loss in our lives,
not for the victorious loved one.**

DAY 8

TOP SECRET

Read Romans 2:1-16.

"This will take place on the day when God will judge men's secrets through Jesus Christ, as my gospel declares" *(v. 16).*

Tennessee officials accused Alabama of having a spy at their practices before the 1954 game. They didn't, but what they did have was a substitute quarterback, and that was more than enough.

The odds favored UT when starting Tide quarterback Bart Starr was unable to play, leaving the game in the hands of a 192-pound junior reserve named Albert Elmore. Elmore proceeded to play so well that one sportswriter declared him to be "the greatest Alabama quarterback in history -- on Shields-Watkins Field." Tennessee tried out a new defense that day, and UT tailback Johnny Majors admitted, "Elmore tore it up."

Elmore got the Tide on the board in the second quarter with an 11-yard toss to halfback Bobby Luna, who added the extra point. Then in the third quarter, Elmore hit halfback Corky Tharp for a seven-yard score and end Nick Germanos for a 25-yard TD. In the fourth quarter, Tharp added a 96-yard interception return to complete the 27-0 rout. Elmore finished his day with three touchdown passes and 107 yards rushing. In a different age, he also "called a near-flawless game."

The defeat was the worst Bama had laid on the Vols since a

CRIMSON TIDE

51-0 whipping back in 1906. Naturally, Tennessee folks looked for a reason for the surprising and thorough whipping. They found it in a claim that Alabama had spied on their practices and thus knew their secrets, including the new defense.

In fact, a "spy" was discovered that week on the Hill overlooking the practice field. Caught red-handed, an Alabama student denied being a spy but confessed that he had "made a bet with some boys back home that I could get into a UT class. And I did it." He also told UT officials how friendly their students were.

We have to be vigilant about the personal information we prefer to keep secret. Much information about us -- from credit reports to what movies we rent -- is readily available to prying and persistent persons. In our information age, people we don't know may know a lot about us — or at least they can find out. And some of them may use this information for harm.

While diligence may allow us to be reasonably successful in keeping some secrets from the world at large, we should never deceive ourselves into believing we are keeping secrets from God. God knows everything about us, including the things we wouldn't want proclaimed at church. All our sins, mistakes, failures, shortcomings, quirks, prejudices, and desires – God knows all our would-be secrets.

But here's something God hasn't kept a secret: No matter what he knows about us, he loves us still.

The secret to success is to start from scratch and keep on scratching.
– Former NFL coach Dennis Green

**We have no secrets before God, and it's no secret
that he nevertheless loves us still.**

ALABAMA

ALL OR NOTHING

Read Deuteronomy 6:4-9.

"Love the Lord your God with all your heart and with all your soul and with all your strength" (v. 5).

Right before two-a-days began, Bear Bryant suddenly burst into song -- or at least a full-fledged holler. That the song he chose was the classic hymn "Love Lifted Me" said much about the man who attempted the singing.

On that dew-brushed August morning in 1981, Bryant began the 24th year of his tenure at Alabama and the 43rd season of his career as a coach. He had first come to Alabama as a player in the fall of 1931 when, he said, "There wasn't but about three cars on campus then." None of the three was his.

At 68, the Bear was an old man. He had overslept that morning he serenaded his boys with a hymn, the first day of the season when he would break Alonzo Stagg's career record for wins. "He can look very old sometimes," said a sportswriter. "He is wrinkled and gray and his coat rides up high on his neck and his pants droop off his seat, and he just shuffles along. He looks, for example, a lot older than the President [Richard Nixon, who was 70]."

"My doctor says I look 10 years younger than last year," Bryant grumbled. "Of course, in the first place, he's lying, and in the second, there's all these pills -- 11 in the morning, alone." Like many old men, Bryant had weak kidneys.

CRIMSON TIDE

"I do get so tired of it at times," the legend admitted in 1981, but he also declared, "I don't want to stop coaching." So why not? He certainly had nothing left to prove. Why did he still do it? "I do love the football," he explained. Love drove him.

All too many sports fans cheer their loudest when their team is winning championships, but they're the first to criticize or turn silent when losses and disappointments come. They're fair-weather fans; their love is conditioned upon winning.

The true Tide fans know that they will love their team and stick with it no matter what, which is exactly the way God commands us to love him. Sure, this mandate is eons old, but the principle it established in our relationship with God has not changed. If anything, it has gained even more immediacy in our materialistic, secular culture that demands we love and worship anything and anybody but God.

Moreover, since God gave the original command, he has sent us Jesus. Thus, we today are even more indebted to God's grace and have even more reason to love God than did the Israelites to whom the original command was given.

God gave us everything, even the life of his only son. In return, we are to love him with everything we have and everything we are. Love is to drive us just as it drove God to a cross and just as it drives God now.

The main thing about staying a coach so long is that you've got to want to.
> -- *Former college football coach Bud Wilkinson*

**With all we have and all we are
– that's the way we are to love God.**

ALABAMA

DAY 10

WATER POWER

Read Acts 10:34-48.

"Can anyone keep these people from being baptized with water? They have received the Holy Spirit just as we have" (v. 47).

Both teams were national championship contenders. A packed house of fans hooted and cheered and generally went berserk. Gamesmanship included the smushing of an orange. Was this Alabama-Tennessee football? Nope. Swimming.

In February 1978, more than 1,200 rabid Tide fans crammed themselves into Alabama's "steamy" natatorium for a swim meet. The two squads were the resident powerhouses of what consisted of SEC swimming back then. Only the season before, the Tide had finished second to Southern Cal for the national championship.

In the SEC, though, UT was king with six straight conference titles. Alabama had finished second three years in succession. All this meant that the rivalry was hotly -- and sometimes bitterly and colorfully -- contested. In a prior meet, Tennessee had purposely tried to lure a freshman Bama swimmer into a false start that would have disqualified him. During a Tide win two seasons before, Alabama Coach Don Gambril had placed the Vol team next to the Tide band and in front of a drafty doorway.

Much more than pride was therefore at stake when the teams met in 1978. The Tennessee swimmers showed up dressed in their customary coonskin caps (and orange swimsuits of course) and

CRIMSON TIDE

engaged in their usual ritual of emptying a bottle of "Big Orange" water into the pool. The crowd hooted, and "an Alabama bruiser in combat boots placed an orange on a starting block and stomped it. The hoots turned to cheers."

Much to the crowd's delight, the Tide prevailed 63-50 over this "most unbeloved college swim team." The tide that February afternoon wasn't orange, big or otherwise; it was crimson.

Children's wading pools and swimming pools in the backyard. Fishing, boating, skiing, and swimming at a lake. Sun, sand, and surf at the beach. If there's any water around, we'll probably be in it, on it, or near it. If there's not any at hand, we'll build a dam and create our own.

We love the wet stuff for its recreational uses, but water first and foremost is about its absolute necessity to support and maintain life. From its earliest days, the Christian church appropriated water as an image of life through the ritual of baptism.

Since the time of the arrival of the Holy Spirit at Pentecost, baptism with water has been the symbol of entry into the Christian community. It is water that marks a person as belonging to Jesus. It is through water that a person proclaims for the world to see and to know that Jesus Christ is his Lord.

For the Christian, water's power lies in the part it plays in granting and sustaining both physical and spiritual life.

Swimmers are like teabags; you don't know how strong they are until you put them in the water.

– Source unknown

There is life in the water:
physical life and spiritual life.

CHANGEOVER

Read Romans 6:1-14.

"Just as Christ was raised from the dead through the glory of the Father, we too may live a new life" (v. 4).

Things changed when Bear Bryant hit town in 1958, and some folks didn't like it very much.

In January 1958, billboards went up around town welcoming Bryant and his wife, Mary Harmon, to Tuscaloosa. "There was a new sheriff in town," and folks were excited about it after three straight miserable seasons. They expected some changes and they got them.

The problem, though, was that Bryant's changes went beyond the football team. His style required adjustments in the greater community at large.

A group of local businessmen who were among the richest Alabama boosters regularly met downtown to play gin and drink coffee. The football coach usually joined them, and then those close to the coach would often go to the coach's office and sit around and visit for a spell. Right away, Bryant laid the law down: "Off-premises is OK, gentlemen. But don't come to the office. . . . I don't come to your office and drink coffee when you're writing a million-dollar loan.' In other words, when Bryant was working, they weren't welcome.

He also stopped the tradition of sharing lengthy lunches with businesspeople and the practice of letting them attend practices.

CRIMSON TIDE

That last one really made some folks mad because Bryant kept them out through the simple expedient of locking the gate.

The changes had some folks griping and fulminating at first, but soon they caught on to what Bryant was doing: "He was building the team. He felt like he was hired to win football games and that was what he intended to do." Ultimately, if the changes meant Alabama stood a better chance of winning, then they were just fine.

Anyone who brashly asserts no change is needed in his or her life isn't paying attention. Every life has doubt, worry, fear, failure, frustration, unfulfilled dreams, and unsuccessful relationships in some combination. The memory and consequences of our past often haunt and trouble us.

Recognizing the need for change in our lives, though, doesn't mean the changes that will bring about hope, joy, peace, and fulfillment will occur. We need some power greater than ourselves or we wouldn't be where we are.

So where can we turn to? Where lies the hope for a changed life? It lies in an encounter with he who is the Lord of all Hope: Jesus Christ.

For a life turned over to Jesus, change is inevitable. With Jesus in charge, the old self with its painful and destructive ways of thinking, feeling, loving, and living is transformed.

A changed life is always only a talk with Jesus away.

Change is an essential element of sports, as it is of life.
-- Erik Brady, USA Today

**In Jesus lie the hope and the power
that change lives.**

DAY 12

YOU NEVER KNOW

Read Exodus 3:1-12.

"But Moses said to God, 'Who am I, that I should go to Pharaoh and bring the Israelites out of Egypt?' And God said, 'I will be with you'" (vv. 11-12a).

You never really know what you can do, but play golf for the first time when you're blind? No way. That's exactly what Charley Boswell thought until he picked up a club.

Boswell played both baseball and football for the Crimson Tide from 1937-39. Sportswriter Clyde Bolton called him "the star" of the Tide's 7-6 upset of Fordham and its legendary Seven Blocks of Granite in 1939. In his three seasons at left halfback for Coach Frank Thomas, Boswell averaged 43.2 yards per punt, a record that stood for more than 30 years.

On Nov. 30, 1944, Cpt. Boswell's tank unit was involved in a firefight and several tanks were disabled and caught fire. "I went in and got a kid out of one of the burning tanks," Boswell recalled. "When I went back to get somebody else, we got hit again and I took a pretty good blast to the face." The explosion threw Boswell clear of the burning tank but left him permanently blinded.

Boswell spent four months in overseas hospitals before he was shipped to the states and a rehab facility in Philadelphia. One day a rehab specialist named Kenny Gleason came into his room and suggested Boswell give golf a try. "I thought it was a joke," Boswell said. But Gleason kept at it until he convinced Boswell he could teach him to play golf.

On a course, Gleason helped Boswell line up his stance, and he promptly drove the ball 200 yards down the middle of the fairway. He was never skeptical again. He went on, in fact, to become a legend by winning 28 blind golf championships, once shooting a round of 81, and scoring a hole-in-one.

You never know what you can do until – like Charley Boswell -- you want to bad enough or until – like Moses -- you have to. Serving in the military, maybe even in combat. Standing by a friend while everyone else unjustly excoriates her. Taking up golf after a debilitating injury. Undergoing agonizing medical treatment and managing to smile. You never know what life will demand of you.

It's that way too in your relationship with God. As Moses discovered, you never know where or when God will call you or what God will ask of you. You do know that God expects you to be faithful and willing to trust him even when he calls you to tasks that daunt and dismay you.

You can with absolute trust respond faithfully to whatever God calls you to do. That's because even though you never know what lies ahead -- and with God you never do -- you do know that God will both lead you and provide what you need.

I told him to get out of the room. I didn't see how in the world I could ever play golf.
-- Charley Boswell's reaction when Kenny Gleason suggested he try golf

You never know what God will ask you to do,
but you always know he will provide everything
you need to do it.

DAY 13

THE PIONEER SPIRIT

Read Luke 5:1-11.

"So they pulled their boats up on shore, left everything and followed him" (v. 11).

James "Lindy" Hood never played basketball in high school and had to be talked into trying out for the Alabama team. Nevertheless, he became one of the game's pioneers when he developed a unique shooting style.

Hood received his nickname after a crowd in New Orleans confused him with famous aviator Charles Lindbergh. He was a football player for Alabama who, because of his size (6'7") and despite his inexperience, drew the attention of basketball coach Hank Crisp. Teammate Ed Kimbrough recalled that Hood "didn't have the ability some of his teammates had. He just worked and worked until he made himself."

Hood was the team's starting center as a sophomore in 1929, and then in 1930 he led the Tide to the only undefeated record in school history. The squad went 20-0 and won the Southern Conference championship. Hood was honored as Alabama's first basketball All-America.

Hood was so tall for his era that his height once resulted in an injury. The architect who designed the Alabama gym apparently never considered that the Tide might have a player as tall as Hood was. He placed the balcony about seven feet from the main floor around the edges of the court. In practice, "the balcony got all mixed up with 'Lindy's' arms and hands," and he lacerated a finger, causing him to miss the 1930 season opener.

While a Stanford player is generally credited with popularizing the one-handed shot in the mid-1930s, Kimbrough asserts that Hood was the first player to shoot with one hand. "That was about the only way he shot," Kimbrough said.

James Hood the reluctant player thus led the game's move into a day when the two-handed set shot was relegated to history.

Going to a place in your life you've never been before requires a willingness to take risks and face uncertainty head-on. You may have never instituted a change in the way a sport is played, but you've had your moments when your latent pioneer spirit manifested itself. That time you changed careers, volunteered at a homeless shelter, learned Spanish, or went back to school.

While attempting new things invariably begets apprehension, the truth is that when life becomes too comfortable and too familiar, it gets boring. The same is true of God, who is downright dangerous because he calls us to be anything but comfortable as we serve him. He summons us to continuously blaze new trails in our faith life, to follow him no matter what. Stepping out on faith is risky all right, but the reward is a life of accomplishment, adventure, and joy that cannot be equaled anywhere else.

Life is an adventure. I wouldn't want to know what's going to happen next.

-- Bobby Bowden

**Unsafe and downright dangerous, God calls us
out of the place where we are comfortable to a life
of adventure and trailblazing in his name.**

ALABAMA

OUT WITH THE OLD

Read Hebrews 8:3-13.

"The ministry Jesus has received is as superior to theirs as the covenant of which he is mediator is superior to the old one, and it is founded on better promises" (v. 6).

Bear Bryant knew it was time for something new; the old stuff just wasn't working anymore.

In both 1969 and '70, the Tide went 6-5, losing to Auburn and Tennessee both years. When Bama tied Oklahoma in the Blue-bonnet Bowl after the 1970 season, "that was the last straw for Coach Bryant. The minute he boarded the plane back to Atlanta from Houston, he had his pencils and paper out, working on a plan." His plan involved what he had just seen in the game: the wishbone offense.

"In the late sixties, we had been throwing the ball a lot," said longtime assistant coach Clem Gryska. This was so even though Bryant was not a big fan of the passing game. He preferred running, blocking, and playing defense.

So after spring practice in 1971, Bryant visited his old friend Darrell Royal, the head coach at Texas. Royal "had been perfecting a new system which was becoming popular in places like Texas and Oklahoma." It was the wishbone. Bryant called and asked if he could spend some time with Royal. As it turned out, the Alabama coach moved in with the Royals, who were temporarily living in an apartment while their home was being renovated.

CRIMSON TIDE

The two coaches set up a projector and went to work, but it didn't take long. After one morning watching film, Bryant told Royal, "You can shut that thing down. I've seen all I need. I've decided to go with the wishbone." Bryant then unveiled his new offense in the '71 season opener against Southern Cal, which had rung up the Tide 42-21 the year before. Alabama won 17-10. "The wishbone was a smash" and the slump was over.

Your car's running fine, but the miles are adding up. Time for a trade-in. Your TV set is still delivering a sharp picture, but those HDTV's are something to see. Maybe even a 3-D set. Hasn't somebody somewhere come out with a smarter cell phone this week? And how about those bodacious lawn mowers that can turn on a dime?

Out with the old, in with the new — we're always looking for the newest thing on the market. In our faith life, that means the new covenant God gave us through Jesus Christ. An old covenant did exist, one based on the law God handed down to the Hebrew people. But God used this old covenant as the basis to go one better and establish a covenant available to the whole world. This new way is a covenant of grace between God and anyone who lives a life of faith in Jesus.

Don't get caught waiting for a newer, improved covenant, though; the promises God gave us through Jesus couldn't get any better.

What's new? Oh, nothing.
— Dialogue between USC and Tide radio announcers before '71 game

God's new covenant through Jesus Christ is plenty old, but don't look for anything better to replace it.

DAY 15

THANKS A LOT

Read 1 Thessalonians 5:12-28.

"[G]ive thanks in all circumstances, for this is God's will for you in Christ Jesus" (v. 18).

As a Christian, Jay Barker's natural attitude was one of gratitude. He was even grateful when he got benched in one of the biggest games of his career.

Barker played quarterback for Gene Stallings from 1991-94, leading the Tide to the 1992 national championship. As a senior in '94, he won the Johnny Unitas Golden Arm Award, emblematic not just of exceptional play on the field but also of outstanding character, scholarship, and leadership. He finished fifth in the Heisman voting. His record as a quarterback at Alabama was 35-2-1, the best percentage (.934) in school history.

When the Tide met Georgia in 1994, the Bulldogs featured strong-armed quarterback Eric Zeier. Barker said, "The coaches told me that Eric was going to throw for three hundred yards, you're going to maybe throw for a hundred." Sure enough, Zeier came out chunking; Barker got benched.

"I was struggling," Barker admitted. So Stallings told his team leader, "You need to sit over here and watch. You need to get your act together and see things clearly."

The unorthodox move worked. Barker came back in to have one of the greatest passing games in Alabama history. With the game in the balance, he hit wide receiver Toderick Malone for a

touchdown, and Bama won 29-28.

Normally a conservative passer, Barker finished the night with an incredible 396 yards passing. He shared his faith with the audience during ESPN's postgame interview and expressed gratitude to Stallings for sitting him down because the benching served to motivate him.

Thank you, Lord, for my cancer. Thank you, Lord, for my unemployment. Thank you, Lord, that my children are in trouble with the law. Is this what the Bible means when it tells us to always be thankful?

Of course not. Being a man of reasonably good sense, Paul didn't tell us to give thanks *for* everything that happens to us, but to give thanks to God even when bad things occur. The joy we know in our soul through Jesus, the prayers we offer to God, and the gratitude we feel for our blessings even in the midst of distress – these don't fluctuate with our mood or our circumstances.

Failure to thank God implies that we believe we alone are responsible for the good things that have come our way. Such an arrogance relegates God to the fringes of our lives. An attitude of gratitude keeps God right where he belongs in our lives: at the heart and soul.

No matter what we may think, we are not self-made men and women.

I just want to thank God for blessing me with some athletic talent and letting me play for the University of Alabama.
-- All-American Linebacker Derrick Thomas

**No matter what happens in our lives,
we can always be thankful for God's presence.**

DAY 16

BONE TIRED

Read Matthew 11:27-30.

"Come to me, all you who are weary and burdened, and I will give you rest" (v. 11).

Mark Ingram was tired. So all he did was pick his team up, put it on his back, and carry it to a win.

On Oct. 17, 2009, against South Carolina, Ingram had already had a great game as the fourth quarter ticked away. He had set a personal high with 178 yards rushing. Unfortunately, he was about all that was working for the Alabama offense. The Tide had little or no passing game, had fumbled four times, and had been penalized ten times for 113 yards.

The defense, however, had limited the No. 22 Gamecocks to two first-half field goals and had scored the game's only touchdown. Safety Mark Barron had intercepted a pass and returned it 77 yards for the score.

Still, with the Tide's offensive woes, Carolina trailed only 13-6 and was very much in the game following a punt to the Alabama 32 with about eight minutes left to play. "Even though they were running for a lot [of] yards, we were right there," said Gamecock coach Steve Spurrier.

The Tide coaches were "looking for the knockout punch. One long, point-producing, time-draining drive" that would be "the effective death knell for the Gamecocks." With no passing attack, that meant one thing: Mark Ingram. Offensive coordinator Jim

CRIMSON TIDE

McElwain decided to see just how far his sophomore tailback, no matter how tired he was, could carry his team.

Pretty far, it turned out. On the first play, Ingram rumbled for 24 yards to the Carolina 44. That was only the beginning. Five more times, Ingram got the call. The result was 44 more yards and a game-clinching touchdown.

Alabama had moved to 7-0 on the back of a tired running back who that night became the frontrunner for the Heisman Trophy.

The everyday struggles and burdens of life beat us down. They may be enormous; they may be trivial with a cumulative effect. But they wear us out, so much so that we've even come up with a name for our exhaustion: chronic fatigue syndrome.

Doctors don't help too much. Sleeping pills can zonk us out; muscle relaxers can dull the weariness. Other than that, it's drag on as usual until we can collapse exhaustedly into bed.

Then along comes Jesus, as usual offering hope and relief for what ails us, though in a totally unexpected way. He says take my yoke. Whoa, there! Isn't a yoke a device for work? Exactly. Our mistake is in trying to do it all alone. Yoke ourselves to Jesus, and the power of almighty God is at our disposal to do the heavy lifting for us.

God's strong shoulders and broad back can handle any burdens we can give him. We just have to let them go.

There were times when I thought about coming out, but I stayed with it.
-- Mark Ingram against South Carolina

**Tired and weary are a way of life
only when we fail to accept Jesus' invitation
to swap our burden for his.**

THE INTERVIEW

Read Romans 14: 1-12.

"We will all stand before God's judgment seat. . . . So then, each of us will give an account of himself to God" *(vv. 10, 12).*

The most successful head coach on the Alabama campus was never interviewed for the job.

Six national championships through the 2013 season. Seven SEC titles. Twenty-eight regional titles. Four times the SEC Coach of the Year and four times the national coach of the year.

That's the record for Sarah Patterson, Alabama's gymnastics head coach. In 2003, she became the sixth female inductee into the Alabama Sports Hall of Fame. She is the longest tenured head coach in Alabama history.

When athletic director Bear Bryant hired Patterson in 1978, such notions of grandeur were an illusion. She was the fifth head coach in five seasons; the size of the crowd at meets depended upon "the number of relatives gymnast Ann Woods Shealy could lure from Anniston."

She was only 22 years old when she dared to challenge Bryant head-on. In the basement of Coleman Coliseum, the rookie coach argued that her program needed a new floor mat. Assistant athletics director Sam Bailey replied that the old wrestling mat she had would do. "With every ounce of conviction she could muster," Patterson declared to Bailey and to a silent Bryant that nothing less than a new $5,000 gymnastics floor would do. That total was equal to her annual salary. Bryant cleared his throat and said, "Sam, give the little lady what she wants."

Bryant actually had hired her without an interview. In effect, Patterson was "a mail-order hire." Fresh out of Slippery Rock, she had interviewed and been hired as an assistant coach when she received a letter in the mail telling her she wasn't an assistant anymore. She had been promoted to head coach.

You know all about job interviews even if you've never had one for a position and been promoted before you even started. You've experienced the stress, the anxiety, the helpless feeling. You tried to appear relaxed, struggling to come up with reasonably original answers to banal questions and to cover up the fact that you thought the interviewer was a total geek. You told yourself that if they turned you down, it was their loss, not yours.

You won't be so indifferent, though, about your last interview: the one with God. A day will come when we will all stand before God to account for ourselves. It is to God and God alone – not our friends, not our parents, not society in general – that we must give a final and complete account. Since all eternity will be at stake, it sure would help to have a surefire character reference with you. One – and only one -- is available: Jesus Christ.

We finished second nationally three years in a row one time, and I got sympathy cards.

-- Sarah Patterson

**You will have one last interview -- with God --
and you sure want Jesus there with you
as a character witness.**

ALABAMA

TEAM PLAYERS

Read 1 Corinthians 12:4-13, 27-31.

"Now to each one the manifestation of the Spirit is given for the common good" (v. 7).

Nick Saban could never pinpoint exactly when the change occurred that transformed a 6-6 season of mediocrity into a 12-0 season of triumph. He just knew it was a team thing.

Saban knew that the attitude and the ethic of the team changed from the end of the 2007 regular season and the beginning of the 2008 season. "It's not something that's a one-time thing," he said. "Character, attitude, and team chemistry are not one-time occurrences." The result was a return to glory marked by an undefeated regular season.

Some players and Saban himself believed the turnaround began during practice for the PetroSun Independence Bowl of Dec. 30, 2007. A "mercurial senior class took a back seat to a united group of underclassmen." Juniors Rashad Johnson and Antoine Caldwell -- and not outgoing seniors -- were named captains for the bowl game.

Johnson said that after the 6-6 season the "team took stock of itself in December and said 'no more.'" He said everybody saw that what they were doing wasn't good enough. "We saw where it got us -- going back to Shreveport," he said. "We needed to make a change."

Alabama defeated Colorado 30-24 in the bowl game, and Saban

praised the team's grit. The players said that win was the catalyst for what followed. Winter workouts improved; attendance at summer's optional drills was 100 percent. Intensity during running and weight lifting increased. Seniors regarded freshmen as teammates rather than competitors for playing time.

The changes were team-wide; so were the results.

Most accomplishments are the result of teamwork, whether it's a college football team, the running of a household, the completion of a project at work, or a dance recital. Disparate talents and gifts work together for the common good and the greater goal.

A church works exactly the same way. At its most basic, a church is a team assembled by God. A shared faith drives the team members and impels them toward shared goals. As a successful Alabama football team must have running backs and offensive tackles, so must a church be composed of people with different spiritual and personal gifts. The result is something greater than everyone involved.

What makes a church team different from others is that the individual efforts are expended for the glory of God and not self. The nature of a church member's particular talents doesn't matter; what does matter is that those talents are used as part of God's team.

Money may be the most important element in modern-day stock car racing, but team chemistry runs a very close second.
— NASCAR's Bill Elliott

A church is a team of people using their various
talents and gifts for God, the source
of all those abilities to begin with.

ALABAMA

ANIMAL HOUSE

Read Genesis 6:11-22; 8:1-4.

"God remembered Noah and all the wild animals and the livestock that were with him in the ark" (v. 8:1).

For the life of him, Don McNeal could not kill Kate no matter how hard he tried.

McNeal grew up on a farm in South Alabama where the kids chopped cotton and picked peas for local farmers. His dad's "farming methods were simple and demanding, but effective." What he had instead of a tractor was a former rodeo star named Kate, a mule he had bought for $75.

When his older brothers grew up, young Don inherited the task of plowing behind Kate. She was a tireless worker; Don was not, so he decided to kill Kate before she worked him to death. He first tried to starve her to death; then he tried "not giving her any water, tried giving her too much water so she'd have heat stroke or something." Nothing worked.

Finally, McNeal settled upon a diabolical plan sure to work. At the end of the day, he loaded Kate in the back of the truck, hit the accelerator, and swerved hard through a 90-degree turn. "The ol' gal flew out of the back of the truck and down an embankment." In the truck, young Don celebrated; "I knew she was done."

He had to act concerned, though, when he joined his dad at the top of the hill. "It was raining cats and dogs and that old mule, to my surprise, was standing up," McNeal recalled. "She turned around and looked right at me like she was saying, 'Don McNeal, don't you ever try that again. I'm going to be with you forever.'"

McNeal finally escaped Kate and the farm through football. The All-American cornerback was part of the 1978 and '79 national champions. He made Alabama's Team of the Century and played ten seasons of pro football.

Through his life, he carried with him the lessons he learned about hard work back on that farm -- and behind Kate.

Do you have a dog or two around the place? How about a cat that passes time staring longingly at your caged canary? Kids have gerbils? Maybe you've gone more exotic with a tarantula.

Americans love our pets with perhaps only a little less fondness for the farm animals that serve as workers, food, and livelihood. We not only share our living space with animals we love and protect but also with some – such as roaches and rats – that we seek to exterminate.

None of us, though, has the problems Noah faced when he packed God's menagerie into one boat. God saved all his varmints from extinction, including the fish and the ducks, who were probably quite delighted with the whole flood business.

The lesson is clear for we who strive to live as God would have us: All living things are under God's care. God doesn't call us to care for and respect just our beloved pets; we are to serve God as stewards of all of his creatures.

I hated Kate. Kate worked us to death.

-- *Don McNeal*

God cares about all his creatures,
and he expects us to respect them too.

ALABAMA

DAY 20

HUMBLE PIE

Read Matthew 23:1-12.

"The greatest among you will be your servant. For whoever exalts himself will be humbled, and whoever humbles himself will be exalted" (vv. 11-12).

Losing to Auburn is bad enough, "but the excruciating part is that you have to endure all those insults for a whole year." The Iron Bowl as much as anything else is a battle for bragging rights.

Contemporary fans should not delude themselves into thinking that the fierceness of the rivalry is anything new. Auburn and Alabama can't even agree on what *season* they played their first game against each other. It was Feb. 22, 1893, but Alabama's records consider it the final game of the 1892 season while Auburn claims it as the first game of the 1893 season. Auburn first pointlessly accused Alabama of cheating in 1894. Disputes over several aspects of the 1908 game led to the cessation of play until 1948.

Alabama quarterback Richard Todd led Bama to a 35-0 pasting of Auburn in 1973 and declared, "I didn't mind all the phone calls cussin' me out for going to Alabama, but it kinda hurt when some of my old high school teachers who are Auburn fans refused to talk to me."

Rubbing Auburn's nose "in the trough is deemed a God-given right" after a victory. "If you live in Alabama," Kenny Stabler once said, "you have to live with Auburn people all year long. So you dish it out when you win because you're going to have to

CRIMSON TIDE

listen to it when you lose. And I don't mean just for the week after the game. I mean until the next one."

No one is immune. Seeking refuge in his cabin on Lake Martin, Bear Bryant was once "buzzed by an armada of boaters squawking, 'War Eagle!'" The only way to shut them up is teach them some humility -- for a year at least -- by winning the Iron Bowl.

We fail to make a sports team or a cheerleading squad. Our children remind us what fossils we are. Though we don't really want to concede the point, there's always somebody younger, smarter, better looking, and more aggressive around. Sometimes it's not very hard being humble, is it?

But Jesus preached that humility is to be a way of life, and he demonstrated what he meant by the manner in which he lived. Humility doesn't demand abject poverty, ongoing afflictions, or a complete lack of social status. Humility, rather, is an attitude toward God and other people.

God calls us in Jesus to be willing servants, always looking for the chance to help others. We banish both thoughts and acts of violence, arrogance, and selfish pride toward others, replacing them with a lifestyle that values peace and harmony.

This is certainly not the way society usually thinks and functions. Moreover, in Jesus' topsy-turvy kingdom, today's servants are tomorrow's exalted.

I'd love to beat Notre Dame, don't get me wrong. But nothing matters more than beating that cow college on the other side of the state.
— Bear Bryant

**To be humbled today in the name of Jesus
is to be exalted forever in the presence of Jesus.**

DAY 21

ORPHANS NO MORE

Read 1 John 3:1-10.

"How great is the love the Father has lavished on us, that we should be called children of God!" (v. 1a)

Interest in Alabama basketball was so lacking in the early days that the team became known as "Alabama's Orphan Five."

The Tide played their first men's basketball game in 1913, an overtime loss to the Bessemer Athletic Club. The campus newspaper had a ready excuse for the loss, claiming, "The University team was greatly handicapped by the low ceiling, many attempted long shots for goal striking the ceiling and bouncing to the floor." The reporter apparently ignored the fact that Bessemer played on the same floor.

That first team went 7-4 for the season, but was not successful at the gate. Only a few paying customers showed up, and the student paper bemoaned, "Owing to the lack of support we may not have a team next year."

The program survived, though, posting winnings records each year through 1916, but the support didn't get any better. Prior to the 1916 season, the *Tuscaloosa News* noticed "the sport's lack of prominence in the town and on the campus."

Basketball took a back seat to practically every other campus activity. For instance, one of the games in 1916 was called "at 7:15 o'clock in order to give time to those desiring to attend the glee club concert." The squad rarely had a full-time coach as players doubled as the coach for several of the early teams.

In 1921, a preseason newspaper story declared, "The University of Alabama athletic followers have been more or less doubtful about basketball in the past." The period of "Alabama's Orphan Five" ended that year, though, because in 1921 Charles Bernier arrived in Tuscaloosa as the athletic director and took on the job of head basketball coach.

Few members of society elicit our sympathy as do orphans, children who through no fault of their own are without parents. This is not just a warm and fuzzy response, though; in the Bible God mandates that we are to care for orphans. Jesus delivered one of his greatest promises shortly before his death when he promised his followers he would not leave them as orphans (John 14:18) but would send the Holy Spirit.

The natural cycle of life decrees that we all are to become orphans when our parents predecease us. In pouring out his great love for us, God declares we will be orphans no more, but instead are his children. In a sense, we are all children of God because he has created us all.

But through Jesus, he means much more: We are in truth his adopted children; he is our father in every good and familial sense of the relationship. Through Christ, we are God's children right now and forever. Welcome to the family!

Students at the university are getting interested in the great winter pastime which is so popular in the North.
-- Alabama student newspaper in 1921 on the end of the 'orphan' era

**Through Jesus Christ, we are adopted
into a father-child relationship with God.**

ALABAMA

DAY 22

THE ALABAMA WAY

Read Romans 13:8-14.

"The night is nearly over; the day is almost here. So let us put aside the deeds of darkness and put on the armor of light" (v. 12).

Onlooking fans probably assumed the coach was comforting his disappointed star quarterback. Much more than that was going on, however. What was really taking place was an indoctrination into The Alabama Way under Bear Bryant.

From 1962-64, Joe Namath quarterbacked the Tide to a 29-4 record and the '64 national championship. Bryant once said that recruiting Namath was "the best coaching decision I ever made" and called him "the greatest athlete I ever coached." In turn, Namath said Bryant was "not only the smartest coach I ever knew, but the man who taught me the meaning of integrity."

But the free-wheeling youngster from Beaver Falls, Penn., had much to learn when he arrived in Tuscaloosa in 1961. He had to learn The Alabama Way, which then, of course, meant the Bear Bryant Way of conducting yourself on and off the field.

For instance, Namath struggled against Vanderbilt in 1962, and Bryant pulled him. Mad at himself for his lousy play, Namath slammed his helmet onto the ground as he headed to the bench. Bryant came over, sat, down, and put what appeared to be a consoling arm around his quarterback.

Not so. "He was nearly squeezing my head off," Namath said

CRIMSON TIDE

later. "'Boy,' he said, 'Don't let me ever see you come out of a game throwing your helmet around and acting like a show-off. Don't ever do that again.'" It wasn't The Alabama Way.

That way also meant doling out discipline to reserves and star quarterbacks alike. Late in the 1963 season, when he was confronted by Bryant, Namath told the truth and confessed to violating team rules. The coach kicked him off the team "for the year. Or forever. Or until you've proved something to me."

Namath made it back, of course, and the result was the perfect 10-0 season of 1964 and the national title. The Alabama Way.

You have a way of life that defines and describes you. You're a die-hard Crimson Tide fan for starters. Maybe you're married with a family. A city guy or a small-town gal. You wear jeans or a suit to work every day. And then there's your faith.

For the Christian, following Jesus more than anything else defines for the world your way of life. It's basically simple in its concept even if it is downright daunting in its execution. You act toward others in a way that would not embarrass you were your day to be broadcast on Fox News. You think about others in a way that would not humiliate you should your thoughts be the plotline for a new CBS sitcom.

You make your actions and thoughts those of love: at all times, in all things, toward all people. It's the Jesus way of life, and it's the way to life forever with God.

I deserved that suspension 100 percent. No, make it 110 percent.
-- Joe Namath on his being kicked off the team his junior season

To live the Jesus way is to act with love
at all times, in all things, and toward all people.

DAY 23

KNOW-IT-ALLS

Read Matthew 13:10-17.

"The knowledge of the secrets of the kingdom of heaven has been given to you" (v. 11).

Billy Neighbors didn't seem to appreciate the importance of education when he was a freshman at Alabama. At least not until Bear Bryant and a school dean ganged up on him.

Neighbors played on both the offensive and defensive lines from 1959-61 and was All-America in 1961. He was stocky and strong and he loved football, so college life on the field was no problem. Off the field, however, was another matter.

"I wasn't doing too well in school," Neighbors admitted. "Matter of fact, I wasn't doing anything. I was cutting classes." Still, when Bryant asked Neighbors to eat lunch with him, "I knew I had a problem, but I didn't know why he was mad. To tell you the truth, I didn't think he knew what kind of grades I was making!"

But Bryant knew exactly what Neighbors was -- or wasn't -- doing. He had the school dean with him and a record of how many classes Neighbors had cut. When the coach started talking, the freshman hung his head until Bryant told him, "Look up at me, boy, I'm talking to you."

Bryant told the dean, "This boy right here can help us win, but if he doesn't start getting better grades, he isn't going to be here." The dean piped up then, reviewing Neighbors' less than stellar academic history.

"I'm going to give him one more semester," Bryant said. "I'm going to move him into my house with me, and I'm going to do him like I do Paul, Jr., when he comes home with a C. I'll beat him with a dictionary!"

"I got straightened out real fast!" Neighbors said.

We can never know too much. We once thought our formal education ended when we entered the workplace, but now we have constant training sessions, conferences, and seminars to keep us current whether our expertise is in auto mechanics or medicine. Many areas require graduate degrees now as we scramble to stay abreast of new discoveries and information. And still we never know it all.

Nowhere, however, is the paucity of our knowledge more stark than it is when we consider God. No matter how much we study, we will never know even a fraction of all there is to apprehend about the creator of the universe – with one important exception. God has revealed absolutely everything we need to know about the kingdom of Heaven to ensure our salvation. He has opened to us great and eternal secrets.

All we need to know about getting into Heaven is right there in the Bible. With God, ignorance is no excuse and knowledge is salvation.

You hear a lot of talk now about education and players getting a degree. Let me tell you something: It was big to Coach Bryant back in 1958.
– Billy Neighbors

When it comes to our salvation, we can indeed know it all because God has revealed to us everything we need to know.

ALABAMA

HUGS AND KISSES

Read John 15:5-17.

"Now remain in my love" (v. 9b).

Alabama softball coach Patrick Murphy used a most unusual recruiting tool to land one of his greatest players ever: He hugged her.

Brittany Rogers completed her career at Alabama with the 2009 season. She was part of a four-year run that included a 221-40 record and three appearances in the Women's College World Series. She was All-America and All-SEC all four seasons. Called by Murphy the "fastest kid we've ever had on the team," Rogers set a school record with 198 career stolen bases. She finished her career second in Alabama softball history with a .417 average, second in runs scored (256), and second in hits (343). In 2009, she won the school's Paul W. Bryant Award as the top female student-athlete.

And all that started with a hug.

Tide assistant coaches Alyson Habetz and Vann Stuedeman scouted Rogers while Murphy was off coaching the Canadian Olympic team. They noticed that she was a hugger, so they tipped Murphy off. "When you meet her, make sure you give her a hug," they said. Murphy noted that, "You know, when you correspond with a kid (by e-mail) for a long time, it's almost like meeting a pen pal."

So when Murphy finally met Rogers, he commented on his

long-lost pen pal and gave her a big hug. That clinched it; she was playing college ball for Alabama. "I come from a very hugging family," Rogers explained. "Every time I see my mom or grandma or anyone, we always give each other a hug."

Considering her success and her team's achievements while she was in Tuscaloosa, Rogers gave and received more than her fair share of exuberant hugs.

That friend from college you haven't seen for a while. Your family, including that aunt with the body odor. We hug them all, whether in greeting, in good-bye, or simply as a spontaneous display of affection. The act of physically clutching someone tightly to us symbolizes how closely we hold them in our hearts.

So whether you are a profligate hugger like Brittany Rogers or a more judicious dispenser of your hugs, a hug is an act of intimacy. Given that, the ultimate hugger is almighty God, who, through Christ, continuously seeks to draw us closer to him in love. A good hug, though, takes two, so what God seeks from us is to hug him back.

We do that by keeping him close in our hearts, by witnessing for his Son through both words and deeds. To live our lives for Jesus is to engage in one long, refreshing, heartwarming, and glorious hug with God.

[Coach Murphy] was the only head coach who came up to me and gave me a bear hug the first time he met me. That won me over.

-- Brittany Rogers

**A daily walk with Christ means
we are so close to God that we are engaged
in one long, joyous hug with the divine.**

DAY 25

GOOD JOB

Read Matthew 25:14-30.

"His master replied, 'Well done, good and faithful servant!'" (v. 21)

Alabama fans the world over will forever remember and recall the famous goal-line stand against Penn State in the 1979 Sugar Bowl. (See Devotion No. 2.) But the Tide pulled off another goal-line stand against Penn State that was so good even Bear Bryant sat up and took notice.

In 1981, Alabama played the Nittany Lions with Bryant trying to win his 314th game, which would tie Amos Alonzo Stagg's record for wins. In the second half, State drove inside the Tide ten. During the sequence, Alabama drew a penalty, so Penn State wound up getting seven snaps from inside the ten, four of them from inside the five.

Okay, maybe a four-play stand. But seven? Nothing to it. That's because, as All-American safety Tommy Wilcox pointed out, they were ready for just such a situation because of the weekly " lower gym workout," better known as "gut-check day." Wilcox recalled that for one hour "you were constantly moving, people barfing in garbage cans, coaches mentally pushing you when you didn't think you could take another step, always screaming, 'Fourth quarter, what ya gonna do? Your back's to the wall, they're on the goal line, they're fixin' to score.'"

So when the Bama defense lined up for play after play against

CRIMSON TIDE

Penn State, for Wilcox and his fellow defenders, "It was just one of those things. 'Been there and done that,' and they're not getting in the end zone." Sure enough, the Tide held. The defense pulled off a seven-play goal-line stand.

Even the Bear was impressed. Wilcox said that as the joyous players reached the sideline, "Coach Bryant took his hat off and tipped it at us, as if to say, 'A job well done, men.'"

That stand keyed a 31-16 Alabama win, and Bryant broke Stagg's record the following week with a win over Auburn.

Good job. Well done. Way to go.

They are words that make us all swell up a little like a puffer fish and smile no matter how hard we try not to. We may deny it in an honest attempt to be at least reasonably humble, but we all cherish praise. We work hard and we may be well rewarded for it financially, but a cold, hard paycheck is not always enough. We like to be told we're doing something well; we desire to be appreciated.

Nowhere, however, is that affirmation more important than when it comes from God himself. We will all meet God one day, which is intimidating even to consider. How our soul will ring with unspeakable joy on that day of days if we hear God's thundering voice say to us, "Well done, good and faithful servant."

Could anything else really matter other than doing a good job for God?

Man, that just sent goosebumps.
-- Tommy Wilcox on Bryant's tip of the hat

**If we don't do a good job for God in our lives,
all our work amounts to nothing.**

IT'S THE TRUTH

Read Matthew 5:33-37.

"Simply let your 'Yes' be 'Yes,' and your 'No,' 'No';
anything beyond this comes from the evil one" (v. 37).

Because his mother spoke the cold, hard truth to him, Alabama kept a player who was to become one of its most successful quarterbacks ever.

Richard Todd started for three seasons (1973-75), sharing duties with Gary Rutledge his sophomore season. He directed the Tide's devastating wishbone offense of the era. The team went 33-3 and won three SEC titles and the 1973 national championship. Alabama never lost an SEC game that Todd started.

In high school, Todd had reservations about the wishbone offense with its emphasis on the run and liked Auburn. On a recruiting trip, Coach Bryant told Todd he would fit well in the wishbone. Todd nevertheless asked Bryant if there were a chance Alabama would pass more out of the wishbone. The Bear's answer was simple: No. Still, Todd ultimately signed with the Tide. "The only reason I went to Alabama was to play for Coach Bryant," he said. "He was the best coach in the country."

In 1972, Todd played his way into the starting position on the freshman team. A loss to Georgia Tech reinforced every misgiving Todd had about playing in a wishbone offense. "I was unhappy after the game," he said. "I didn't like the offense. I hadn't played very well, and I was really down."

CRIMSON TIDE

That's when his mother, a former college basketball player, showed up. He whined to her that he wished he hadn't gone to Alabama, that the offense didn't suit him, and that he should transfer to another school that didn't run the wishbone and help them win. His mother bluntly replied, "The way you played today, you wouldn't have helped anyone else, either."

She wasn't going to let her despondent son blame the offense for the loss, so she spoke the truth. By the spring, he was ready.

No, that dress doesn't make you look fat. But, officer, I wasn't speeding. I didn't get the project finished because I've been at the hospital every night with my ailing grandmother. What good-looking guy? I didn't notice.

Sometimes we lie to spare the feelings of others; more often, though, we lie to bail ourselves out of a jam, to make ourselves look better to others, or to gain the upper hand over someone.

But Jesus admonishes us to tell the truth. Frequently in our faith life we fret about what is right and what is wrong, but we can have no such ambivalence when it comes to whether we should tell the truth or we should lie.

God and his son are so closely associated with the truth that lying is ultimately attributed to the devil ("the evil one"). Given his character, God cannot lie; given his character, the devil lies as a way of life. Given your character, which is it?

Trampling on the truth has become as common place as overpaid athletes and bad television.

-- Hockey coach Dan Bauer

**Jesus declared himself to be the truth,
so whose side are we on when we lie?**

DAY 27

CONTROL FREAK

Read Luke 1:57-79.

"[F]or you will go on before the Lord to prepare the way for him, to give his people the knowledge of salvation" (vv. 76b-77a).

Alabama coach Dave Rader pounded on the window in the press box in a desperate attempt to get his quarterback's attention. There was nothing he could do, though. What was about to happen was out of his control.

"How stupid is that?' Rader asked about his frantic attempts to get quarterback Brodie Croyle's attention from his seat high above Bryant-Denny Stadium. "Like Brodie's going to hear me."

What got Rader so frantic was what he saw on the field as the Tide lined up on third and goal at the Arkansas five-yard line. On Sept. 24, 2005, Alabama led Arkansas only 17-13 in the fourth quarter when Rader and head coach Mike Shula had the team in the I formation for a draw play.

Tide receiver D.J. Hall saw the same thing Rader did: Nothing. Across from him was nobody. "I was shocked to see I was out there by myself," Hall said. That's what Rader saw; the draw play wouldn't work but getting the ball to Hall would. But whether or not Croyle saw the defense was out of Rader's control.

As it turned out, Croyle did see it. He glanced at Hall, who tapped his helmet. Croyle nodded. At the snap, he didn't hand the ball to fullback Kenneth Darby, who was still expecting the

ball. Instead, he tossed it to a wide-open Hall, who hauled it in for the game-clinching touchdown in the 24-13 victory.

When Croyle saw the botched coverage, he didn't want to tip off his knowledge so he looked only once in Hall's direction. "I didn't want to look out [at Hall] again," he said. Unlike Dave Rader, he was in control all the way.

Maybe your children hang out with kids you don't particularly like. Your mother has joined a motorcycle club. The Tide loses a key SEC game. Vexing, isn't it?

But you might as well face it: You can't control the people you love. You can't control what they do from day to day, and you can't control their relationship with God.

While we certainly want the ones we care about to number themselves among Jesus' disciples, we aren't responsible for their ultimate eternal destination, thank the Lord. In other words, we can't save anyone else, and God hasn't given us that awesome responsibility. Only God through Jesus Christ saves.

We are in control of and responsible for our own salvation. When it comes to others, we follow in the footsteps of John the Baptist by making sure they know of the salvation God offers through his son. We tell them of Jesus; the rest is between them and God.

You have no control over what the other guy does. You only have control over what you do.
-- World Cup skier A.J. Kitt

While God is in control of an individual's
salvation, we are commanded to give him
the knowledge of Christ he needs to be saved.

ALABAMA

NO TURNING BACK

Read Colossians 3:5-17.

"You have taken off your old self with its practices and have put on the new self" (vv. 9-10).

In the winter of 2009, Alabama added a new starting quarterback -- to its baseball team.

Athletes moving from one school to another is commonplace. A player moving from one SEC school to another is rarer. What Chris Smelley did on Jan. 12, 2009, is even more atypical. After three seasons as a starting quarterback for South Carolina, he transferred to Alabama -- and the baseball team.

Smelley never originally intended to give up baseball when he arrived in Columbia, but it wound up that way as he focused on the demands of playing quarterback in college football's best league. He didn't tire of football; "in the end, I just felt like this was the thing I needed to do," he said, adding that he was back doing "what makes me the most happy."

It certainly was a big change. This was a player who knew success at the highest level of collegiate competition. On Oct. 4, 2008, he completed 22 of 37 passes for 327 yards in a 31-24 win over Ole Miss only a week after the Rebels had defeated eventual national champion Florida.

Because of an NCAA rule about athletes transferring in the middle of a school year, Smelley had to sit out the 2009 baseball season. And there he was as the 2010 season began, battling for playing time as a catcher before a crowd of about 1,000 instead of the tens of thousands he had played before in Columbia.

There he was, too, after an 8-7 win over Nicholls State, pushing a broom to sweep sunflower seeds into a pile in the Tide dugout, one of the less-than-glamorous chores rookies must do. After rounding up a big pile, he looked up and smiled. He had made a move from which he could not turn back, and he was perfectly delighted about the whole business.

Courageous pioneers seeking a better life spread out across unfamiliar territory and in the process conquered the American wilderness. That wanderlust seems part of our national character now, and you probably inherited it. A new job, a new home, better schools for the kids -- you'll load up a U-Haul truck or the back of a pickup and head out to a new place for any number of reasons. As Chris Smelley did, you leave the old behind and embrace the new, knowing you can never turn back -- and not wanting to.

An encounter with Jesus Christ has a similar effect on a person's life. You leave behind the old ways; new habits beckon. You move on to a different, new, and even unfamiliar you with no desire to ever again be what you were before.

Jesus never gives you the option of turning back, so with your eyes and your heart fixed on the road ahead, you set out for bigger, better, and more glorious days.

I loved playing for Coach [Steve] Spurrier and the Gamecocks. But I'm here now.

-- *Chris Smelley*

An encounter with Jesus Christ sets a life on a road to glory from which there is no turning back.

DAY 29

NOT WHAT THEY SEEM

Read Habakkuk 1:2-11.

"Why do you make me look at injustice? Why do you tolerate wrong? Destruction and violence are before me; there is strife, and conflict abounds" (v. 3).

Hey, the move from the college game to the professional ranks is a step up, a promotion to the big time, right? Not for Alabama guard John Hannah it wasn't.

At the height of Hannah's pro career, a *Sports Illustrated* cover story dubbed him "The Best Offensive Lineman of All Time." Bear Bryant may have agreed, once proclaiming Hannah "the best offensive lineman I ever coached." Hannah was a key component of the Tide turnaround of 1971-72 when, after two lackluster seasons, Bryant switched to the wishbone offense. (See Devotion No. 14.) Alabama went 21-3 and won two SEC championships.

After his All-American career in Tuscaloosa, Hannah moved on to a pro career where he achieved fame and success rare for an offensive lineman. The New England Patriots drafted him in the first round in 1973, and he started immediately. He played in Super Bowl XX, a blowout loss. Hannah later called not getting a Super Bowl ring the biggest disappointment of his career.

He made the AFC Pro Bowl team ten times and was the league's Offensive Lineman of the Year four straight times. He was the first Patriot to be inducted into the Pro Football Hall of Fame.

So all that glitz of being in the pros must have dazzled Hannah,

CRIMSON TIDE

right? Actually, he found it to be "a step down from Alabama." When a newspaper writer asked the rookie how it would feel to be playing in front of 55,000 people, Hannah said, "It won't be too disappointing." The guy looked at him as though he were nuts until Hannah explained: "You've got to remember, I've been playing in front of 80,000 people for the last three years."

Even in pro football, things just aren't always what they seem.

Sometimes in life things aren't what they seem either. In our violent and convulsive times, we must confront the possibility of a new reality: that we are helpless in the face of anarchy; that injustice, destruction, and violence are pandemic in and symptomatic of our modern age. It seems that anarchy is winning, that the system of standards, values, and institutions we cherish is crumbling while we watch.

But we should not be deceived or disheartened. God is in fact the arch-enemy of chaos, the creator of order and goodness and the architect of all of history. God is in control.

We often err in that we misinterpret history as the record of mankind's accomplishments -- which it isn't -- rather than as the unfolding of God's plan -- which it is. That plan has a clearly defined end: God will make everything right. In that day things will be what they seem.

Unlike any other business in the United States, sports must preserve an illusion of perfect innocence.

-- Author Lewis H. Lapham

The forces of good and decency often seem helpless before evil's power, but don't be fooled: God is in control and will set things right.

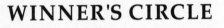
DAY 30

WINNER'S CIRCLE

Read 1 John 5:1-12.

"Who is it that overcomes the world? Only he who
believes that Jesus is the Son of God" (v. 5).

Alabama fans on Dec. 3, 1957, weren't really hoping for much.
They just wanted to win again. What they got was "glory days at
Alabama beyond [their] wildest reckoning."

From 1955-57, Tide fans suffered through what has been called
"The Dark Years." Under J.B. "Ears" Whitworth, a lineman who
played for both Wallace Wade and Frank Thomas, Alabama won
only four games in three seasons. Whitworth was described as
"a nice guy who was put into an impossible situation," but "the
bottom line was that things were *bad*."

Thus, on Dec. 3, 1957, university officials announced that Paul
"Bear" Bryant would be the new head football coach at Alabama.
From the first, Bryant's emphasis was on winning. "I came here
to make Alabama a winner again," he told his players at an early
meeting.

Lineman Dave Sington recalled that Bryant told them, "I'm not
worried about whether I'm going to win or lose. I know I'm going
to win. . . . The only thing I don't know is how many of you in
this room are winners." That was during the time when players
showed up for practice and apprehensively saw the walls of the
gymnasium lined with garbage pails for vomiting.

The winning began with the first season and never stopped

CRIMSON TIDE

under Bryant. While two coaches have won more major college games than the Bear did, "no college football coach built winning football teams better than Bryant." From 1958 through 1982, the Tide won six national championships and 13 SEC titles. Alabama had 25 winning seasons and played in 24 consecutive bowls. The only season the Tide went bowlless was Bryant's first, when he declined an invitation from the new Bluegrass Bowl.

"When the whistle blew for the first spring practice in 1958, Bama was on track to a return to glory" -- and winning.

Life itself, not just athletic events, is a competition. You vie against all the other job applicants. You compete against others for a date. Sibling rivalry is real; just ask your brother or sister.

Inherent in any competition or any situation in which you strive to win is the involvement of an antagonist. You always have an opponent to overcome, even if it's an inanimate video game, a golf course, or even yourself.

Nobody wants to be numbered among life's losers. We recognize them when we see them, and maybe mutter a little prayer that says something like, "There but for the grace of God go I."

But one adversary will defeat us: Death will claim us all. We can turn the tables on this foe, though; we can defeat the grave. A victory is possible, however, only through faith in Jesus Christ. With Jesus, we have hope beyond death because we have life.

With Jesus, we win. For all of eternity.

I ain't nothing but a winner.

-- Bear Bryant

Death is the ultimate opponent;
Jesus is the ultimate victor.

DAY 31

THE FAME GAME

Read 1 Kings 10:1-10, 18-29.

"King Solomon was greater in riches and wisdom than all the other kings of the earth. The whole world sought audience with Solomon" (vv. 23-24).

Hundreds of autograph seekers pressed against a chain-line fence, reached out their hands, and called his name, begging for his attention. Not bad for a guy who was rumored to be dead before the season began.

At a school renowned for its legendary quarterbacks, Brodie Croyle ranks among Alabama's best. His 2,499 passing yards in 2005, his senior season, were the highest in a single season in Bama history. He set a school record that season by throwing 190 passes without an interception. He led the Tide to a 10-2 record, a No. 8 ranking, and a win in the Cotton Bowl.

Before he did all that, though, the rumor circulated that he had been killed in a preseason hunting accident in Argentina. One version said Croyle and his dad had been killed in a car wreck; another said they had died after being kidnapped. Fortunately for Alabama fans, Croyle returned to Tuscaloosa quite alive and quite recovered from the torn ligament that had sidelined him for most of the 2004 season.

The apex of both Croyle's career and his fame at Alabama probably occurred on Oct. 8, 2005, when he led the Tide to a 31-3 rout of No. 5 Florida. He "made seemingly every throw in the

book," completing 14 of 17 throws for 283 yards and three TDs.

In the waning minutes of the game, the fans descended upon the chain-link fence back of the Alabama bench. "The throng had eyes for only the Ringo Starr look-alike with the mop-top 'do, beseeching him with cries of 'Bro-deee!'" The reaction to Croyle was called "Beatlemania-like."

Have you ever wanted to be famous? Hanging out with other rich and famous people, having folks with microphones listen to what you say, throwing money around like toilet paper, meeting adoring and clamoring fans, signing autographs, and posing for the paparazzi before you climb into your imported sports car?

Many of us yearn to be famous, well-known in the places and by the people that we believe matter. That's all fame amounts to: strangers knowing your name and your face.

The truth is that you are already famous where it really does matter, which excludes TV's talking heads, screaming teenagers, moviegoers, or D.C. power brokers. You are famous because the Almighty God of the universe knows your name, your face, and everything about you.

Ponder that for a moment and then ask yourself: If a persistent photographer snapped you pondering this fame – the only kind that has eternal significance – would the picture show the world unbridled joy or the shell-shocked expression of a mug shot?

We just try to be as nice as we can and keep moving.
– Brodie Croyle's dad, John, on the crush of fans

You're already famous because
God knows your name and your face,
which may be either reassuring or terrifying.

DAY 32

EXCUSES, EXCUSES

Read Luke 9:57-62.

"Another said, 'I will follow you, Lord; but first let me go back and say good-by to my family'" (v. 61).

Everybody else was making excuses. All the Crimson Tide did was go out and win the tournament.

SEC basketball coaches were understandably not too pleased when the 1982 conference basketball tournament was held at Rupp Arena in Lexington. The LSU coach called the site "a disgrace to integrity" and suggested a more neutral court would have been "Leningrad Stadium." The Ole Miss coach was quite upset about the officiating, perhaps with good reason. In losing to Kentucky, his team was whistled for an unbelievable 38 fouls, each one of which led his players and him to smell a "home-cooked rat." The coach was so upset, in fact, that he broke down and cried about the whole deal.

While everybody else was whining and complaining, the Tide went out and stunned Kentucky in the finals with a masterly game plan and some tenacious rebounding. What Coach Wimp Sanderson did was eliminate the much-bewailed advantage of the homecourt and the home crowd by slowing the game down. Never mind that the Tide had averaged 78 points a game during the season.

The two teams battled even during the last half. With the score tied at 46, Kentucky got the ball out, but Mike Davis and freshman guard Ennis Whatley forced a traveling call with 24 seconds left to play. "Get the ball airborne quick," Sanderson instructed Whatley since the Cats had a foul to give. But Whatley managed to elude a foul and then let fly as the clock wound down. His jumper missed, but he snared his own rebound and fired again. Air ball. Senior forward Eddie Phillips grabbed the ball and flipped it into the hole as the game ended.

No excuses. Just a win and an NCAA Tournament berth.

Has some of your most creative thinking involved excuses for not going in to work? Have you discovered that an unintended benefit of computers is that you can always blame them for the destruction of all your hard work? Don't you manage to stammer or stutter some justification when a state trooper pulls you over? We're usually pretty good at making excuses to cover our failures or to get out of something we don't particularly want to do.

Sadly, that holds true for our faith life also. The Bible is just too hard to understand so I won't read it; the weather's too pretty to be shut up in church; praying in public is embarrassing and I'm not very good at it anyway; Sunday's the only day I have to sleep in late. We're good at making excuses to justify ourselves before God. The plain truth is, though, that whatever excuses we make for not following Jesus wholeheartedly are not good enough.

Jesus made no excuses to avoid dying for us; we should offer none to avoid living for him.

There are a thousand reasons for failure but not a single excuse.
-- Former NFL Player Mike Reid

Try though we might, no excuses can justify
our failure to follow Jesus wholeheartedly.

THE NEW YOU

Read 2 Corinthians 5:11-21.

"If anyone is in Christ, he is a new creation; the old has gone, the new has come!" (v. 17)

He can sell tickets too." Thus did Bear Bryant describe what may well be the most versatile football player in the program's history.

Bryant delivered his only slight exaggeration on his television show while watching the highlights of the previous day's game. The player he spoke of was David Ray.

Ray came to Alabama after a rather unusual recruiting ploy Bryant pulled. Following the 1960 season, Florida head coach Ray Graves was actually at Ray's home to sign him to a scholarship Ray had already said he would accept. That's when Alabama assistant coach Elwood Kettler called to tell Ray it was *withdrawing* its scholarship offer because Bryant had said he didn't believe Ray was good enough to play at Alabama.

Whether Bryant was sincere or was simply pulling a psychological ploy remains unknown. What happened, though, is that Ray instantly changed his mind. He signed with Alabama "to prove them wrong."

Ray was certainly good enough to play for the Tide. He was All-America in 1964 when he led the nation in scoring and the Tide in interceptions. He also kicked a field goal that was the difference in a 17-14 win over Florida.

CRIMSON TIDE

So he played offense, defense, and special teams, right? Yes, he did, but his versatility ran deeper than that. While at Alabama, Ray played defensive back, halfback, split end, defensive end, and tight end and also punted and placekicked. "I didn't care where I played, just as long as I was playing," Ray said. "I really didn't have a favorite position."

David Ray continually made himself over as a football player depending on what the team needed at the time.

Ever considered a makeover? TV shows have shown us how changes in clothes, hair, and makeup and some weight loss can radically alter the way a person looks.

The problem is that those changes are only superficial; they're only skin deep. Even with a makeover, the real you — the person inside — remains unchanged. How can you make over that part of you? In other words, how can you really discover a new you?

By giving your heart and soul to Jesus -- just as you give up your hair to the makeover stylist. You won't look any different; you won't dance any better; you won't suddenly start talking any smarter. Rather, the change is on the inside where you are brand new because the model for all you think and feel is now Jesus. He is the one you now care about pleasing.

Made over by Jesus, you realize that gaining his good opinion — not the world's — is all that really matters. And he isn't the least interested in how you look but how you act.

You played wherever you could play that would help the team.
-- David Ray

Jesus is the ultimate makeover artist; he can make you over without changing the way you look.

ALABAMA

DAY 34

CELEBRATION TIME

Read Luke 15:1-10.

"There is rejoicing in the presence of the angels of God over one sinner who repents" (v. 10).

Only once in his Alabama career did Steadman Shealy celebrate after a play. And why not? He had just pulled off what is officially recognized as one of the greatest plays in Tide football history.

Despite being a high-school star who was heavily recruited, Shealy had one of the shortest recruiting efforts Bear Bryant ever pulled off. In 1976, Doug Barfield, Auburn's new head coach, was in the Shealys' living room delivering his pitch. Georgia's Vince Dooley was in a car in the driveway waiting his turn. The phone rang; it was Bryant.

Shealy said hello, and Bryant growled, "What jersey have you always wanted to wear?" "Crimson," Shealy replied. "What's the problem then?" Bryant asked. That was it; Shealy was headed to Tuscaloosa to play football.

Shealy quarterbacked the tide during the last three seasons of the 1970s. The team was 34-2 during that run, winning three SEC titles and two national titles.

The Iron Bowl of 1979 was a typical knock-down-drag-out. Alabama was ranked No. 1, but Auburn was ranked also. The Tigers took advantage of several Tide fumbles to score two last-half touchdowns and lead 18-17 with about eight minutes to play.

CRIMSON TIDE

But the Tide offense rallied to score in seven plays, the last one coming from the eight yard line. On the play, Shealy held the ball on the wishbone option and raced around the end, "the quickest 8 yards I've ever seen." That's when he celebrated for the one and only time: "I jumped up, and I patted the football, and the other guys came over and celebrated too." Alabama won 25-18.

A book published several years later labeled Shealy's touchdown run as the 13th greatest play in Tide football history.

Alabama just whipped Auburn. You got that new job or that promotion. You just held your newborn child in your arms. Life has those grand moments that call for celebration. You may jump up and down and scream in a wild frenzy or share a quiet, sedate candlelight dinner at home -- but you celebrate.

Consider then a celebration that is actually beyond anything we can imagine, one that fills every niche and corner of the very home of God and the angels. Imagine a celebration in Heaven, which also has its grand moments. They are touched off when someone comes to faith in Jesus. Heaven itself rings with the joyous sounds of the singing and dancing of the celebrating angels. Even God rejoices when just one person – you or someone you have introduced to Christ? -- turns to him.

When you said "yes" to Christ, you made the angels dance.

Celebrate what you've accomplished, but raise the bar a little higher each time you succeed.

-- *Mia Hamm*

**God himself joins the angels
in heavenly celebration when a single person
turns to him through faith in Jesus.**

HEAD GAMES

Read 1 Peter 1:10-16.

"Prepare your minds for action" (v. 13).

The most highly recruited prospects to ever come to Alabama." So declared Tide women's basketball coach Rick Moody about Niesa Johnson and Yolanda Watkins. Still, he said, they had to get tougher -- between their ears -- to be successful.

Johnson's arrival in Tuscaloosa in the fall of 1991 marked the beginning of the greatest run in the history of the Bama women's program. Watkins arrived a year later. During the 1990s, the Tide women had eight straight seasons of at least twenty wins. They went to the NCAA Tournament each season and advanced to the Sweet 16 four straight times. The highlight of the whole run came in 1994 with a 26-7 season that saw Johnson, a junior, and Watkins, a sophomore, lead the team to the Final Four.

Johnson was All-America both as a junior and a senior. Watkins joined her as All-SEC. The latter was a 6-2 power player with both strength and quickness. Johnson relied on her quickness and a deadly shot from 3-point range. She didn't have that shot when she started out. At her first game with the YMCA when she was 9, she discovered she couldn't shoot at all, but that she was really fast. So she shot layups all game. She blocked shots, chased the ball down, and then outran everybody to the basket. She scored 52 of her team's 54 points.

But neither player came to Tuscaloosa perfect. Moody said his two stars had all the physical talents, but they had to get mentally tough to succeed in the SEC. He knew Watkins was there when she injured her knee in the Midwest Regional championship game against Penn State in 1994. He thought she was lost for the season with a knee injury, but she stayed on the bench only long enough for the trainer to straighten out her knee. Then she tapped Moody on the shoulder and told him she was ready to go.

Tough enough, thank you.

Once upon a time, survival required mere brute strength, but persevering in American society today generally necessitates mental strength rather than physical prowess.

Your job, your family, your finances -- they all demand mental toughness from you by placing stress upon you to perform. Stress is a fact of life, though it isn't all bad as we are often led to believe. Stress can lead you to function at your best. Rather than buckling under it, you stand up, make constant decisions, and keep going.

So it is with your faith life. "Too blessed to be stressed" sounds nice, but followers of Jesus Christ know all about stress. Society screams compromise; your children whine about being cool; your company ignores ethics. But you don't fold beneath the stress; you keep your mind on Christ and the way he said to live because you are tough mentally, strengthened by your faith. After all, you have God's word and God's grace for relief and support.

Football is more mental than physical, no matter how it looks from the stands.

-- Former NFL Linebacker Ray Nitschke

**Toughened mentally by your faith in Christ,
you live out what you believe, and you persevere.**

DAY 36

THOSE THINGS

Read Isaiah 55:6-13.

"For my thoughts are not your thoughts, neither are your ways my ways" (v. 8).

It was just one of those things, and the result was Crimson Tide legend.

On April 29, 2009, Woodrow Lowe figured the package UPS had delivered was just another autograph request. So when he got around to scanning the letter that accompanied the football, he was in for a big surprise. It read: "Congratulations from the National Football Foundation." Woodrow Lowe had been elected to the College Football Hall of Fame.

"I was stunned," Lowe said. He was probably the only one.

From 1972-75, Lowe wreaked havoc on SEC offenses as a Crimson Tide linebacker. He and Cornelius Bennett are the Tide's only three-time football All-Americas. During his time in Tuscaloosa, Lowe's play was the source of a statement uttered repeatedly on Sunday afternoons in the fall. Weekly on his TV show, Bear Bryant would declare, "That tackle is by Woodrow Lowe of Phenix City, a fine young man."

And until one of "those things" happened, Lowe was headed to nearby Auburn to ply his talents. A teammate and he were invited by the Tigers to visit and watch a game. His friend "had a beat-up old car, and we got a flat tire on the way over there," Lowe recalled. They didn't have a spare either. They had to hitchhike to Auburn, and the game was over by the time they arrived. They didn't see any Auburn coaches, who, probably figuring Lowe wasn't interested, never contacted him again.

And yet, Lowe said, 'If they had called back, I probably would have gone there." It was just one of those things that seemed like a bad break to Lowe at the time.

You've probably had a few of "those things" in your own life: bad breaks that occur without regard to justice, morality, or fair play. When those things happen, more often than not they leave you wondering if everything in life is random with events determined by a chance roll of some cosmic dice. Is there really somebody scripting all this with logic and purpose?

Yes, there is; God is the author of everything.

We know how it all began; we even know how it all will end. It's in God's book. The part we play in God's kingdom, though, is in the middle, and that part is still being revealed. The simple truth is that God's ways are different from ours. After all he's God and we are not. That's why we don't know what's coming our way, and why "those things" catch us by surprise and dismay us when they do occur.

What God asks of us is that we trust him. As the one – and the only one – in charge, he knows everything will be all right for those who follow Jesus.

Sometimes the calls go your way, and sometimes they don't.
-- Olympic gold medalist Dr. Dot Richardson

**Life confounds us because, while we know the
end and the beginning of God's great story, we are
part of the middle, which God is still writing.**

DAY 37

GOOD-BYE

Read John 13:33-38.

"My children, I will be with you only a little longer" (v. 33a).

On the day Gene Stallings said good-bye, his team gave him the perfect going-away gift: a win that was a defensive slugfest all the way.

On Jan. 1, 1997, the 16th-ranked Tide whipped 15th-ranked Michigan 17-14 in the Outback Bowl. The win marked the end of the Stallings era as he had previously announced his retirement as Alabama head coach. His record was 70-16-3, an average of ten wins a season that included a national championship.

Stallings' swan song was fitting for a defensive guru and a disciple of Bear Bryant as his defense carried the day. Michigan led 6-3 early behind quarterback Brian Griese and threatened to blow the game open with another touchdown. But Alabama linebacker Dwayne Rudd stepped in front of a Griese pass for the interception, and he knew what to do with the ball once he had it. He took off down the Michigan sideline behind a convoy of blockers for an 88-yard touchdown.

Rudd would honored as the game's Most Valuable Player. "I didn't see the whole play, but I saw the ball," he said. "I saw some green, and I ran to it."

The Tide never trailed again. The second Alabama touchdown came when the team was trying to run out the clock. Leading

10-6, Alabama kept giving the ball to Shaun Alexander, who kept breaking tackles and picking up yardage. He ultimately burst off the left side for a 46-yard run that made it 17-6 with 2:15 left.

Michigan tried a furious rally with a touchdown and an onside kick, but receiver Chad Goss corralled the ball to wrap up the win. "I can't think of a more fitting game than this for Alabama and Michigan," Stallings said as he left the field for the last time on the shoulders of his players.

You've stood on the curb and watched someone you love drive off, or you've grabbed a last-minute hug before a plane leaves. Maybe it was a child leaving home for the first time or your best friends moving halfway across the country. It's an extended – maybe even permanent – separation, and good-byes hurt.

Jesus felt the pain of parting too. Throughout his brief ministry, Jesus had been surrounded by and had depended upon his friends and confidantes, the disciples. About to leave them, he gathered them for a going-away supper and gave them a heads-up about what was about to happen. In the process, he offered them words of comfort. What a wonderful friend he was! Even though he was the one who was about to suffer unimaginable agony, Jesus' concern was for the pain his friends would feel.

But Jesus wasn't just saying good-bye. He was about his mission of providing the way through which none of us would ever have to say good-bye again.

They say money talks. The only thing it says to me is good-bye.
– Baseball Hall of Famer Paul Waner

**Through Jesus, we will see the day
when we say good-bye to good-byes.**

ALABAMA

MIRACLE PLAY

Read Matthew 12:38-42.

"He answered, 'A wicked and adulterous generation asks for a miraculous sign!'" (v. 39)

Was it divine intervention -- and thus a miracle -- or a coincidence that inspired the Tide to simply maul a bigger, stronger Nebraska team in the 1967 Sugar Bowl? Decide for yourself.

Alabama went 11-0 in 1966. The Tide missed their third straight national title largely because both the UPI and AP decided to name their champions before the bowl games. It wouldn't matter anyhow to Alabama, or so all the experts claimed. The Tide was up against a Nebraska team that was bigger, stronger, and a prohibitive favorite.

The weather didn't help Alabama either. A slight but steady rain had been falling all weekend long in New Orleans. A wet field clearly gave Nebraska another advantage since they ran the ball better than Alabama did.

But that's when the miracle(?) occurred. As quarterback Ken Stabler recalled it, "So, we're coming out of the locker room. It had been drizzling all weekend but I swear, when Coach Bryant stepped on the field it quit raining! It did!"

Then as Stabler walked down the sideline getting ready for the first play of the game, Bryant "was smoking one of his unfiltered Chesterfields and looking out from under that houndstooth hat." He said to his quarterback, "Stabler, I want you to throw the ball, throw it as far as you can on the very first play."

So that's what Stabler did. He hit Ray Perkins on a down and out and the play went for forty-five yards. "We scored six or seven plays later," Stabler remembered. "For all practical purposes, the game was probably over."

Alabama won in a 34-7 cakewalk, the game probably over the moment Bryant stepped onto the field and the rain stopped.

Like a sudden change in the weather that changes the shape of a football game, miracles defy rational explanation. How about escaping with minor abrasions from an accident that totals your car? Or recovering from an illness that seemed terminal? Underlying the notion of miracles is that they are rare instances of direct divine intervention that reveal God.

But life shows us quite the contrary, that miracles are anything but rare. Since God made the world and everything in it, everything around you is miraculous. Even you are a miracle.

Your life thus can be mundane, dull, and ordinary, or it can be spent in a glorious attitude of childlike wonder and awe. It depends on whether or not you see the world through the eyes of faith. Only through faith can you discern the hand of God in any event; only through faith can you see the miraculous and thus see God.

Jesus knew that miracles don't produce faith, but rather faith produces miracles.

I'm no miracle man. I guarantee nothing but hard work.
— Bear Bryant

Miracles are all around us,
but it takes the eyes of faith to see them.

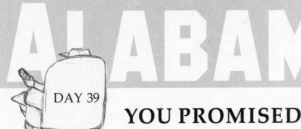

YOU PROMISED

Read 2 Peter 1:3-11.

"He has given us his very great and precious promises, so that through them you may participate in the divine nature" (v. 4).

An Alabama basketball player kept a promise to an injured teammate, and the result was the SEC championship.

In the SEC's early years, the thirteen schools didn't play everyone else during the regular basketball season, so a tournament decided the league championship. The Kentucky Wildcats won the first championship in 1933 and went 11-0 in the conference the second season. The Tide went 16-2 with both of the losses to Kentucky.

The pundits picked Kentucky and LSU to meet in the tourney finals, especially after Alabama's leading scorer, Zeke Kimbrough, suffered a fractured cheekbone in practice and underwent surgery, which sidelined him for the tournament. Kimbrough was the SEC's third leading scorer with 162 points for the season.

The squad dropped by the hospital to tell Kimbrough goodbye. They all cheerfully told him not to worry, that they were going to win the tournament for him. But Jimmy Walker, Kimbrough's "inseparable friend" and the conference's fifth leading scorer, returned to his teammate's bedside after everyone else had left. "We *are* going to win it for you," he said. "That's a promise – and I don't break promises."

As it turned out, Kimbrough got to join his teammates when school president Dr. George Denny made arrangements for the trip. Kimbrough sat on the bench and had his picture made with the team – the team that kept Jimmy Walker's promise.

The Tide beat Mississippi State easily, edged Tennessee by three, and then bombed Florida 41-25 for the title. Walker was the leading scorer in the championship win.

Promise made; promise kept.

What if you and everyone around you lived by that simple but powerful precept: Any promise made is a promise that will be kept? It would certainly change your life, wouldn't it? In fact, it would change the world.

We are sometimes harsh with others who make promises to us and then don't deliver, but we're often guilty of the same short-coming. We all made promises easily and glibly, but when it comes time to deliver – well, such matters as convenience and time come into play. I know I promised, but I didn't really mean it.

God doesn't operate that way. One scholar, who apparently had too much time on his hands, has determined that the Bible contains more than 30,000 promises. Peter calls them "very great and precious," primarily because they came from God but also because God keeps them and they mean for us a life shared with Jesus Christ and all the eternal blessings that entails.

Bear Bryant kept his promise to me. He didn't have white players or black players at Alabama. He just had football players.
--Sylvester Croom, Alabama's first black offensive lineman

God cannot do everything;
he cannot, for instance, break a promise.

DAY 40

TEST CASE

Read James 1:2-12.

"Blessed is the man who perseveres under trial, because when he has stood the test, he will receive the crown of life that God has promised to those who love him" (v. 12).

Frank Thomas had impeccable credentials, and Wallace Wade highly recommended him. Still, he lived and worked every day at Alabama with the knowledge that he was always taking a test.

After his resignation in 1930, Wade recommended Thomas, saying he "should become one of the greatest coaches in the country." Thomas was a backfield coach at Georgia who had played under Knute Rockne at Notre Dame, who called Thomas "one of the smartest players he ever coached." "I don't believe you could pick a better man," Wade told school president George H. Denny.

Denny was the visionary who had seen football as a way for the university to grow in stature and in reputation. It was said that "he was the first [university] president to look at the big picture -- to really look ahead past the season at hand." He was the one who first decided Alabama would be a football power. Thus, he was always actively involved in the process of hiring a new coach.

So on July 15, 1930, Denny met with Thomas and promptly "threw down the gauntlet." "Material is 90 percent, coaching ability 10 percent," Denny declared. Denny told Thomas he would

CRIMSON TIDE

be provided with the 90 percent and that he would "be held to strict accounting for delivering the remaining 10 percent."

A slightly stunned Thomas subsequently asked a newsman if he thought Denny's figures were right. The man replied that the numbers might be off "but there is no doubt the good doctor means what he says."

Thus, Thomas' entire career at Alabama was one long test that he ultimately aced. Denny did his part and fortunately for Alabama, so did Thomas. He coached for 15 seasons and won 115 games, two national championships, and four SEC titles.

Life often seems to be one battery of tests after another: high-school and college final exams, college entrance exams, the driver's license test, professional certification exams. They all stress us out because they measure our competency, and we fear that we will be found wanting.

But it is the tests in our lives that don't involve paper and pen that often demand the most of us. That is, like Frank Thomas, we discover that our abilities and our persistence are regularly tested by the challenges, obstacles, and barriers we run into.

Life itself is one long test, which means some parts are bound to be hard. Viewing life as an ongoing exam may help you keep your sanity, your perspective, and your faith when troubles come your way. After all, God is the proctor, but he isn't neutral. He even gave you the answer you need to pass with flying colors; that answer is "Jesus."

Those were the hardest and coldest words I ever heard.
-- Frank Thomas after his meeting with Dr. Denny

Life is a test that God wants you to ace.

DAY 41

THE LIKENESS

Read Philippians 3:7-11.

*"I want to know Christ and the power of his resurrection
and the fellowship of sharing in his sufferings, becoming
like him in his death" (v. 10).*

Rolando McClain shared a brain with Coach Nick Saban. Or
so it seemed.

In 2009, McClain was first-team All-America and the SEC
Defensive Player of the Year. He led the national champions with
105 tackles and 14.5 stops for losses. He won the Dick Butkus and
the Jack Lambert awards as the nation's top collegiate linebacker.

His teammates were the ones who came up with the notion
of McClain sharing gray matter with the Tide head coach. "Just
picture coach Saban being huge and able to play football," said
All-American cornerback Javier Arenas.

Even Saban noticed similarities in the way the two think. "I'm
a perfectionist, and I think he's a perfectionist," he said. "He likes
to get things right."

McClain often acted as a surrogate for Saban on the field. When
linebacker Dont'a Hightower was injured in the Arkansas game in
2009, Saban had to move several players around. McClain simply
took over on the field, looking "like an orchestra conductor as he
made sure each player knew his assignment for the rest of that
game." The defense held the SEC's top offense to 30 points below
its season average in the 35-7 win.

CRIMSON TIDE

Perhaps McClain's uncanny ability to channel Saban was best illustrated when players prepared to dump a bucket of Gatorade on Saban's head as time ran out in the SEC championship game. McClain stopped them. "It wasn't the right time for it," he said, telling his teammates, "You can put whatever you want to put on him" after the national championship. He knew that Saban would think as he did: that all the goals weren't achieved yet.

Every one of us is like someone else in that we all have people we look up to and – sometimes even unconsciously – model our behavior, our looks, even our conversation after. Athletes, movie stars, TV personalities – to our horror, these are often the people our children want to be like.

But what about adults? Do we, too, sometimes emulate such often unworthy role models? And where can we find someone who is truly worthy of being like?

The answer is blazingly obvious: Jesus Christ. Easily said and impossibly done, but what makes the Christian life both so challenging and so exciting is that we will never become. We will always be about the spiritual task of becoming.

That is, we can never look around us and declare with great satisfaction and smugness, "Today, I am exactly like Jesus." We can, though, humbly give thanks to God that today we are a little more like Jesus than we were yesterday and less like him than we will be tomorrow.

We have a low tolerance for guys who don't know what to do.
-- Rolando McClain explaining how Coach Saban and he think alike

**The Christian life is a lifelong process
of becoming more like Jesus.**

DAY 42

GOAL ORIENTED

Read 1 Peter 1:3-9.

"For you are receiving the goal of your faith, the salvation of your souls" (v. 9).

Stephen Bolt had a clear goal: "Four-zero-zero." Achieving it was hard enough, but then even the SEC coaches conspired to keep him from it.

Bolt was obsessed with those three numbers; he even had them plastered all over his apartment. He chased those numbers all over the country. They were the goal of his life. The numbers stood for four minutes and zero seconds, the holy grail for serious milers. In 1976, Tide runner Bolt was a serious miler.

In 2009, Bolt was inducted into the Alabama Sports Hall of Fame. He was a three-time All-American at Alabama and was the first American runner in history to clock both a sub-four-minute mile and a sub-2:15 marathon.

That four-zero-zero goal was still in front of him, however, at the 1976 SEC Championships. He had run a 3:58 mile on a relay leg the previous week and "knew I was ready to break the four-minute mark. I was so excited." But UA's track coach, John Mitchell, had some bad news for his star. The other coaches had voted to implement a qualifying heat for the mile that would be run the night before the final. According to Bolt, Mitchell said everybody was calling the change the "Steve Bolt Rule." Said Bolt, "They were trying to wear me down so I couldn't run all the events."

At least not well enough to crack that four-minute mile. Bolt's position on the team meant he had to run the two mile and a distance relay before qualifying for the mile, all within 24 hours. Bolt admitted he couldn't see any way that he could run all those events and then be in any shape to reach his four-zero-zero goal.

He had no strategy; he simply ran as fast as he could in everything. He won the two-mile, helped to win the relay, qualified for the mile, and then broke the tape at 3:59:4. Goal achieved!

What are your goals? Have you ever thought them out as Stephen Bolt did? Or do you just shuffle along living for your next paycheck and whatever fun you can seek out instead of pursuing some greater purpose?

Now try this one: What is the goal of your faith life? You go to church to worship God. You read the Bible and study God's word to learn about God and how God wants you to live. But what is it you hope to achieve? What is all that stuff about? For what purpose do you believe that Jesus Christ is God's son?

The answer is actually quite simple: The goal of your faith life is your salvation, and this is the only goal in life that matters. Nothing you will ever seek is as important or as eternal as getting into Heaven and making sure that everybody you know and love will be there too one day.

Looking back, I realize how important it all was in terms of a life lesson: the discipline, the focus, the goals.

-- Stephen Bolt

**The most important goal of your life
is to get to Heaven and to make sure those you
know and love will join you there one day.**

DAY 43

SWEET WORDS

Read John 8:1-11.

"'Then neither do I condemn you,' Jesus declared. 'Go now and leave your life of sin'" (v. 11).

John David Phillips was uncertain about what he had just done until God sent him affirmation of his decision.

Phillips came to Alabama in 1994 as a highly recruited quarterback and played in all twelve games as a defensive back his freshman season. The coaches moved him to wide receiver as a sophomore. Practice went well; he was in the rotation. But, Phillips said, "I had been praying, unable to sleep at night and didn't have peace in my heart about my role on the team." So he made an appointment to see Coach Gene Stallings.

He told Stallings that after much prayer he believed God wanted him to play quarterback. Stallings replied that the move meant he would be redshirted, which Phillips expected. "Well, I think that's a smart move," the coach said.

So Phillips went into the office a playing wide receiver and came out a redshirted quarterback. As he walked toward his car, he thought, "God, I hope I just made the right decision. I just hope that is what you wanted me to do. I need some affirmation."

He got it. Tony Johnson, a tight end and a devoted Christian, walked by before Phillips could get into his car. He came over to Phillips and said he wanted to talk to him. "You may find this odd," he said, "but I just feel like God wants you to play quarterback." He said he had been praying and reading his Bible the night before when God had spoken to him. "I just feel I needed to share that with you."

John David Phillips now knew that his decision was one God wanted him to make.

You make a key decision. All excited, you tell your best friend or spouse and anxiously await for a reaction. "Boy, that was dumb" is the answer you get.

A friend's life spirals out of control into disaster. Drugs, alcohol, affairs, unemployment. Do you just pretend you don't know that messed-up person or do you step in to help?

Everybody needs affirmation in some degree. That is, we all occasionally need someone to say something positive about us, to assert that we are worth something, and to remind us that God loves us. Tony Johnson did that for John David Phillips and in the process eased his uncertainty.

The follower of Jesus does what our Lord did when he encountered someone whose life was a shambles. Rather than seeing what a person were, he saw what the person could become.

Life is hard; it breaks us all to some degree. To be like Jesus, we see past the problems of the broken and the hurting and envision their potential, understanding that not condemning is not condoning.

That was pretty amazing how God used Tony [Johnson], a godly teammate, to affirm my decision.

-- John David Phillips

**The greatest way to affirm lost persons
is to lead them to Christ.**

DAY 44

LESSON LEARNED

Read Psalm 143.

"Teach me to do your will, for you are my God" (v. 10).

What Bear Bryant learned from an experience in a restaurant in South Alabama served him well during his career.

In 1958, long before integration, the Bear was on a recruiting trip when he went into a restaurant "and every head in the place turns to stare at me. Seems I'm the only white fella in the place." The food smelled good, though, so Bryant took a seat.

"A big ole man in a tee shirt and cap" told Bryant, "You probably won't like it here. Today we're having chitlin's, collard greens and black-eyed peas with cornbread. I'll bet you don't even know what chitlin's are." Bryant replied, "I'm from Arkansas. I've probably eaten a mile of them. Sounds like I'm in the right place." When the man brought Bryant's lunch, they started talking. The coach explained he was the new coach at Alabama and was looking for a recruit. The man gave him directions to the local school.

As Bryant left, the man asked if the coach had a photograph he could hang on the walls to show he had been there. Bryant didn't, but he wrote the man's name and address on a napkin and promised to send him one. Back in the office, he found a picture, and wrote on it, "Thanks for the best lunch I've ever had."

Years later, after integration, Bryant recruited an offensive lineman from the area who told him he had his heart set on Auburn. Two days later, the kid called Bryant and told him he

CRIMSON TIDE

would play for Alabama if they still wanted him. Bryant asked him what had changed his mind. "My grandpa," he said. "You ate in his restaurant and you sent him a picture that's his pride and joy. You kept your word to him, and to Grandpa, that's everything. He said you could teach me more than football and I had to play for a man like you."

Bryant said he learned again "that it don't cost nothing to be nice" and that it costs a lot to break your word to someone.

Learning about anything in life requires a combination of education and experience. Education is the accumulation of facts that we call knowledge; experience is the acquisition of wisdom and discernment, which add purpose and understanding to our knowledge.

The most difficult way to learn is trial and error: dive in blindly and mess up. The best way to learn is through example coupled with instructions: Someone goes ahead to show you the way and writes down all the information you need to follow.

In teaching us the way to live godly lives, God chose the latter method. He set down in his book the habits, actions, and attitudes that make for a way of life in accordance with his wishes. He also sent us Jesus to explain and to illustrate.

God teaches us not just how to exist but how to live. We just need to be attentive students.

I was floored. I learned that the lessons my mama taught me were always right. It don't cost nothing to be nice.
– Bear Bryant on being told about the photograph in the restaurant

To learn from Jesus is to learn what life is all about and how God means for us to live it.

DAY 45

HAVE A HEART

Read Matthew 6:19-24.

"Store up for yourselves treasures in heaven. . . . For where your treasure is, there your heart will be also" (vv. 20, 21).

When Jim Wells retired in 2009 as Alabama's head baseball coach, it wasn't the first time. In 2007, he had stepped down for six days before he had a change of heart.

Wells left the Tide dugout as the winningest coach in school baseball history. He led Alabama for fifteen seasons, compiling a 625-322 record. He coached the Tide to three appearances in the College World Series including a runner-up finish in 1997. His teams also won SEC titles in 1996 and 2006, won six SEC tournament championships, and made twelve NCAA regional tournament appearances.

Wells' retirement was "swift, self-effacing and seamless." He even hand-picked his successor, assistant coach Mitch Gaspard.

Maybe the change was so easy because Wells had practice at retiring. In June 2007, he abruptly resigned. Athletics Director Mal Moore tried to talk him into staying on at least through the 2008 season, but Wells was adamant. "After having several conversations with Jim over the last few days," Moore said, "it became evident to me that he feels strongly about this decision."

Not strongly enough, as it turned out. Wells' retirement lasted only six days. On Wednesday after he had retired on Thursday,

CRIMSON TIDE

he met with Moore again and told his boss he had had a change of heart. Moore apparently wasn't too surprised; he had not been in a big hurry to name a replacement.

What happened, plain and simple, was that Wells realized he had made a mistake. "I haven't slept in six days," he said. "I saw how much I missed it." By Monday, Wells said, his heart was leading him to change his mind. "I realized what I had after I let it go, and I wanted to get it back."

So in 2007, Jim Wells retired and then unretired because he had a change of heart. In 2009, he knew in his heart that this time it was time.

As Jim Wells did, we often face decisions in life that force us to lead with our heart rather than our head. Our head says take that job with the salary increase; our heart says don't relocate because the kids are doing so well. Our head declares now is not the time to start a relationship; our heart insists that we're in love.

We wrestle with our head and our heart as we determine what matters the most to us. When it comes to the ultimate priority in our lives, though, our head *and* our heart tell us it's Jesus.

What that means for our lives is a resolution of the conflict we face daily: That of choosing between the values of our culture and a life of trust in and obedience to God. The two may occasionally be compatible, but when they're not, our head tells us what Jesus wants us to do; our heart tells us how right it is that we do it.

I knew the decision wasn't right.
-- Jim Wells about his 2007 retirement

**In our struggle with competing value systems,
our head and our heart lead us to follow Jesus.**

DAY 46

THE MOTHER LODE

Read John 19:25-30.

"Near the cross of Jesus stood his mother" (v. 25).

Dwight Stephenson was wavering on his commitment to Alabama until his mama laid down the law.

Stephenson's mother and father worked relentlessly and tirelessly to provide a good life for their seven children. His dad worked in the Virginia shipyards; his mom worked in the school cafeteria. "She worked hard," Stephenson said of his mother. "When my mother finally retired from her job, she had something like 200-300 sick days she never used."

Dwight's senior year, the college recruiters came knocking on the Stephensons' door. He and two of his teammates made a pact that they would all sign with Alabama together. "Of all the schools that recruited me, Alabama was no question the biggest program," Dwight said. But still, "It seemed like an awful long way [from home] for me, that's for sure."

Thus, when coaches Ken Donahue and John Mitchell showed up to sign the trio, Dwight said he wasn't ready to sign yet. The dismayed coaches then learned that the other two players had changed their mind and signed with NC State.

"As soon as I got home," Dwight said, "I went into the kitchen to see my mama. . . . I told her, 'Mama, I'm going to NC State.' At that point, my mama said, 'You aren't gonna follow anybody anywhere. You're going to the University of Alabama.'"

That ended that discussion. Stephenson walked back into the living room and signed on the dotted line with the Tide.

He became the starting center as a sophomore in 1977. He played on two national champions and was All-SEC and All-America in 1979. He won the Jacobs Trophy as the SEC's best blocker and went on to a Hall-of-Fame career in the NFL.

Thanks to his mama's putting down her foot.

Mamas often work hard and tirelessly and sacrifice personal happiness for the sake of their children. No mother in history, though, has faced a challenge to match that of Mary, whom God chose to be the mother of Jesus. Like mamas and their children throughout time, Mary experienced both joy and perplexity in her relationship with her son.

To the end, though, Mary stood by her boy. She followed him all the way to his execution at Calvary, an act of love and bravery since Jesus was condemned as an enemy of the Roman Empire no matter how arbitrary and unjust the verdict may have been.

But just as mothers like Mary and Dwight Stephenson's mama -- and perhaps yours -- would apparently do anything for their children, so will God do anything out of love for his children. After all, that was God on the cross at the foot of which Mary stood, and he was dying for you, one of his children.

Everyone should find time to write and to go see their mother. I think that's healthy.

-- Bear Bryant

Mamas often sacrifice for their children, but God, too, will do anything out of love for his children, including dying on a cross.

DAY 47

ALL IN

Read Mark 12:28-34.

"Love the Lord your God with all your heart and with all your soul and with all your mind and with all your strength" (v. 30).

I'm just too full of Alabama."

Those were the wistful words of Tommy Lewis, a player who loved Alabama so much that he pulled off one of the most notorious plays in college football history.

Lewis played fullback for three seasons for the Tide, scoring two touchdowns in the 61-6 pasting of Syracuse in the 1953 Orange Bowl. He scored the game's first touchdown in the 1954 Cotton Bowl to jump Alabama out to a 6-0 lead. He is most famous, however, for another play he made in the second quarter.

Rice's star running back was apparently headed for a 95-yard touchdown run when Lewis flattened him with a devastating tackle. The crowd of more than 75,000 gaped in silence. A Rice cheerleader only a few feet away yelled, "He did it! He did it!" Even the TV and radio announcers were "momentarily mute."

The problem was that Lewis had been sitting on the Alabama bench without a helmet. He had turned to a teammate as the Rice back broke into the clear and said, "He's going all the way." His buddy replied, "Yeah, he sure is, Lew." And then the runner was in front of Lewis "and I unloaded on him. I didn't want to lose. It was my last game at Alabama."

CRIMSON TIDE

The referees awarded Rice the touchdown.

After the game, Lewis went to the Rice locker room and apologized, telling the Rice runner he blindsided, "I don't know what got into me." The *Dallas Morning News* the next morning absolved him of any malicious intent, calling him a "genuine competitor" and his infamous play a "forgivable error."

Tommy Lewis just had too much Alabama in him.

What fills your life, your heart, and your soul so much that you sometimes just can't help what you do? We all have a zeal for something, whether it's Alabama football as it was for Tommy Lewis, or whether it's sports cars, jogging, our family, scuba diving, or stamp collecting.

But do we have a zeal for the Lord? Saturday afternoon, we may well jump up and down, scream, holler, even cry – generally making a spectacle of ourselves – when Alabama scores. Yet on Sunday morning, if we go to church at all, we probably sit there showing about as much enthusiasm as we would for a root canal.

Of all the divine rules, regulations, and commandments we find in the Bible, Jesus made it crystal clear which one is number one: We are to love God with everything we have. All our heart, all our soul, all our mind, all our strength.

If we do that, our zeal and enthusiasm will burst forth. Like Tommy Lewis, we just won't be able to help ourselves.

The ingrained philosophy at Alabama was to give a little more than you've got.
-- Young Boozer, halfback on 1934 national champions

The enthusiasm with which we worship God
reveals the depth of our relationship with him.

DAY 48

DANCING MACHINE

Read 2 Samuel 6:12-22.

"David danced before the Lord with all his might, while he and the entire house of Israel brought up the ark of the Lord with shouts and the sound of trumpets" (vv. 14-15).

The win was so important that even Tide head coach Nick Saban danced in celebration.

On Nov. 29, 2008, the Crimson Tide crushed Auburn 36-0 in the Iron Bowl, the most lopsided game in the series since Bama's 38-0 thrashing of the Tigers in 1962. The whipping was so thorough that one reporter called it "the Beatdown in TTown." The Tide rolled up 412 yards of total offense, 253 in the second half, which topped Auburn's output of 170 yards for the whole day.

After the game, Tide players celebrated on the field, some players raising their helmets, others waving the school flag. Saban took a victory lap before heading to the locker room. What was it about this particular game that set off such a celebration? It's not as though the Tide hadn't beaten Auburn before.

Well, they hadn't for a while. Auburn had won six straight games in the bitterly contested series. The win was especially sweet for the nine seniors on the team. "Our goal was to beat Auburn," said safety Rashad Johnson. "We spent six years in a hole. That was our biggest goal."

Saban perhaps expressed best the importance of the win after the series of losses. He said the seniors "should always be recognized as the group that had a tremendous lot to do with changing the culture here." That is, they bought into "the culture" of winning football.

And, yes, rumor has it that in the Alabama locker room the normally dour Saban led his team in singing the fight song and then followed that up with a victory jig.

One of the more enduring stereotypes of the Christian is of a dour, sour-faced person always on the prowl to sniff out fun and frivolity and shut it down. "Somewhere, sometime, somebody's having fun – and it's got to stop!" Many understand this to be the mandate that governs the Christian life.

But nothing could be further from reality. Long ago King David, he who was hand-chosen by God to rule Israel and who would eventually number Jesus Christ among his descendants, set the standard for those who love and worship the Lord when he danced in the presence of God with unrestrained joy.

Many centuries and one savior later, David's example reminds us today that a life spent in an awareness of God's presence is all about celebrating, rejoicing, and enjoying God's countless gifts, including salvation in Jesus Christ.

Yes, dancing can be vulgar and coarse, but as with David, God looks into our hearts to see what is there. Our very life should be one long song and dance for Jesus.

I didn't get to see him dance. We need to get that on YouTube.
-- Rashad Johnson on Nick Saban's victory jig

**While dancing and music can be
vulgar and obscene, they can also be
inspiring expressions of abiding love for God.**

ALABAMA

DAY 49

I TOLD YOU SO

Read Matthew 24:15-31.

"See, I have told you ahead of time" (v. 25).

Mark Gottfried looked his team right square in their collective eyes and told them something they might not have believed at that particular moment: You're going to win this game.

It sure didn't look like it at the time. The occasion was a second-round game in the 2004 NCAA Tournament. Those players to whom Gottfried declared a win had missed 16 of their previous 17 shots. They were getting killed on the boards as their opponent was gradually pulling away, leading by thirteen points with only 7:42 left in the game. Oh, and that opponent? Just the top-seeded Stanford Cardinal.

Well, somebody must have believed Gottfried no matter how improbable his statement. The Tide at least hit something after the time out when Evan Brock nailed a pair of free throws. Then Kennedy Winston followed with a long three-pointer. That shot "was big," Gottfried said. "It took the lid off for our team and gave them confidence again."

Earnest Shelton then hit a three-point bomb. Brock and forward Chuck Davis made a pair of free throws. Antoine Pettway drained yet another three-pointer. That made fifteen straight points, and suddenly to everyone's surprise -- especially Stanford's -- Alabama led 55-53 with only 4:04 remaining. When Winston added another free throw, the Tide had come out of that time out with a

16-0 run and a three-point lead.

A Brock dunk with 2:49 left was the only field goal Alabama made the rest of the way, but they salted away the upset and the amazing comeback by hitting 12 of 16 free throws in the last 1:33. The Tide won 70-67, advancing to the Sweet Sixteen for the first time since 1991 and the Wimp Sanderson days.

And Coach Mark Gottfried told them so.

Don't you just absolutely hate it when somebody says, "I told you so"? That means the other person was right and you were wrong; that other person has spoken the truth. You could have listened to that know-it-all in the first place, but then you would have lost the chance yourself to crow, "I told you so."

In our pluralistic age and society, many view truth as relative, meaning absolute truth does not exist. All belief systems have equal value and merit. What I believe, even if its source is junk some crackpot made up, is as valid as what you believe.

But this is a ghastly, dangerous fallacy because it ignores the truth that God proclaimed in the presence and words of Jesus.

In speaking the truth, Jesus told everybody exactly what he was going to do: come back and take his faithful with him. Those who don't listen or who don't believe will be left behind with those four awful words, "I told you so," ringing in their ears and wringing their souls.

It gives you inspiration when your captain still believes in you. If he says we can win it, that means we can win it.
-- Chuck Davis on Mark Gottfried's statement that they would win

Jesus matter-of-factly told us what he has planned:
He will return to gather all the faithful to himself.

ALABAMA

DAY 50

BELIEVE IT

Read John 3:16-21.

*"For God so loved the world that He gave His only
begotten Son, that whoever believes in Him should not
perish but have everlasting life" (v. 16 NKJV).*

Who would ever have believed it? The SEC championship
game came about because of a bunch of Division II schools up
north, and the Alabama players didn't really want to play in the
first game.

At the 1987 NCAA Convention, the West Chester State athletic
director sought permission to hold season-ending playoff games
in the 14-team Pennsylvania State Athletic Conference and in the
12-member Central Intercollegiate Athletic Association. In sanc-
tioning the conferences' title games, the NCAA in effect decreed
that any league with at least twelve members could hold a championship game after the regular season.

It didn't take long for the SEC's powers-that-be to "recognize a
juicy loophole when [they] saw one." Say hello to Arkansas and
South Carolina as new members of the SEC, Eastern and Western
divisions, and the SEC championship game.

That first game was held in Birmingham on Dec. 12, 1992. 11-0
No. 2 Alabama met No. 12 8-3 Florida. Hard as it may be to believe,
the Tide players grumbled about having to play the game, seeing
themselves as playing for a championship they had already won.
"If it weren't for this newfangled title game," groused defensive

CRIMSON TIDE

end John Copeland, "we could be sitting around playing cards, thinking about [No. 1] Miami" (and the Sugar Bowl and the national championship). "All I know is, we've got practice this week," grumbled linebacker Michael Rogers.

With the score tied in that inaugural title game, Antonio Langham returned an intercepted pass 26 yards for a touchdown and the 28-21 final score. Alabama was the SEC champion and eventually the national champion. That you can believe.

What we believe underscores everything about our lives. Our politics. How we raise our children. How we treat other people. Whether we respect others, their property and their lives.

Often, competing belief systems clamor for our attention; we all know persons – maybe friends and family members – who lost Christianity in the shuffle and the hubbub. We turn aside from believing in Christ at our peril, however, because the heart and soul, the very essence of Christianity, is belief. That is, believing that this man named Jesus is the very Son of God and that it is through him – and only through him – that we can find forgiveness and salvation that will reserve a place for us with God.

But believing is more than simply acknowledging intellectually that Jesus is God. Even the demons who serve Satan know that. It is belief so deep that we entrust our lives and our eternity to Christ. We live like we believe it – because we do.

Like most men, he wrestled with demons and genuinely believed in God.
-- Writer Richard Scott on Bear Bryant

**Believe it: Jesus is the way – and the only way –
to eternal life with God.**

DAY 51

BE PREPARED

Read Matthew 10:5-23.

"I am sending you out like sheep among wolves. Therefore be as shrewd as snakes and as innocent as doves" (v. 16).

Alabama Coach Xen Scott once prepared his team for an opponent by taking them to a football game -- that didn't feature the upcoming opposition.

In 1922, the Tide played a game that would ultimately cast the national spotlight on Alabama for the first time. The opponent was John Heisman's Pennsylvania team, and nobody gave the Tide a chance. After all, Georgia Tech had beaten Alabama 33-7, Navy had beaten Tech 13-0, and Penn had beaten Navy 13-7.

Travel also contributed to the lack of respect for the Tide. They had to travel 2,500 miles to Austin to play Texas, back to Tuscaloosa, and then to Philadelphia to play two games in eight days. The team traveled by train, which "was something, with the cinders blowing through the train cars."

Scott "was a thinker, one of the brainiest coaches in the South." After coaching Alabama in the fall, he went north in the summer to cover horse racing for a Cleveland paper. He knew his boys would probably be overawed by the reputation of Eastern football. So he had the team stop in Washington, D.C., and attend the Navy-Penn State game, which the Midshipmen won 14-0. This masterpiece of psychological strategy left the Alabama players convinced they could play with these Eastern guys.

CRIMSON TIDE

They could. Before the largest crowd ever to watch an Alabama football game, Pooley Hubert's fumble into the end zone was recovered by Clyde "Shorty" Propst for a third-quarter touchdown and a 9-7 Bama win.

Southern football had been vindicated, thanks in large part to Xen Scott 's unique pregame preparations.

You know the importance of preparation in your own life. You went to the bank for a car loan, facts and figures in hand. That presentation you made at work was seamless because you practiced. The kids' school play suffered no meltdowns because they rehearsed. Knowing what you need to do and doing what you must to succeed isn't luck; it's preparation.

Jesus understood this, and he prepared his followers by lecturing them and by sending them on field trips. Two thousand years later, the life of faith requires similar training and study. You prepare so you'll be ready when that unsaved neighbor standing beside you at your backyard grill asks about Jesus. You prepare so you will know how God wants you to live. You prepare so you are certain in what you believe when the secular, godless world challenges it.

And one day you'll see God face to face. You certainly want to be prepared for that.

It's not the will to win that matters; everyone has that. It's the will to prepare to win that matters.

-- Bear Bryant

**Living in faith requires constant study
and training, preparation for the day
when you meet God face to face.**

DAY 52

SOUND OFF

Read Revelation 4:1-10, 5:6-14.

"Then I looked and heard the voice of many angels, numbering thousands upon thousands, and ten thousand times ten thousand" (v. 11a).

Included among the characters of the 1954 Alabama basketball team was a player who used shock and awe among his weapons. He yelled at the opposing players.

When Johnny Dee came south from Notre Dame in 1953, he brought championship basketball with him. He also brought an entire team that became known in Tide lore as The Rocket Eight. At Notre Dame, Dee typically brought about fifty kids from all over the nation in to scrimmage against the Irish varsity. The best got scholarship offers. When Dee landed the Bama job, he simply called up the best of the bunch who hadn't made the cut and brought them South.

The flamboyant Irishman was a master motivator who went 68-25 in his four seasons in Tuscaloosa, including a sensational 21-3 record in 1956. Center Jerry Harper was All-America in both 1955 and '56; forward George Linn earned the honor in '56.

Dee's 1954 team, which went 16-8, included a player "with a slightly different approach to basketball. Billy Crews would remove his false front tooth and practice making disquieting faces. On the court, he added yelling to his facial distortions."

Presumably with a straight face, unlike Crews', Dee explained his player's shenanigans. "A basketball player operates on five senses," he said. "If we can short-circuit two of these senses, the man's only operating with 60 percent efficiency."

The Birmingham News called Crews "the Lon Chaney of Bama's basketballers," saying he looked like "just another Joe College in classes." On the court, though, "he's a sight." And a sound.

Bryant-Denny Stadium erupts in a cacophony on game day. Loud music blares from the rattling speakers in the car next to you at the traffic light. The garbage men bang the cans around as though they receive bonuses for waking you up. A silence of any length in a conversation makes us uncomfortable; somebody please say something.

We live in a noisy world, which means activity, busyness, progress, and engagement with life. The problem with all that noise – however constructive it may be – is that it drowns out God's gentle voice. Though he certainly could, God doesn't bother competing with all that man-made racket. Thus, some quiet time each day is absolutely imperative if we are to grow in our relationship with God. The intentional seeking of silence in which to hear God's voice constitutes surrender to the divine.

Though much about Heaven will be strange, we should be quite comfortable there. Revelation's lengthy description of God's home makes it very clear that it's a noisy place reverberating with the inspiring, exhilarating, and awesome sound of worship.

You can tell a good putt by the noise it makes.
-- Pro Hall-of-Fame golfer Bobby Locke

Heaven is a quite noisy place, echoing constantly
with the wonderful sounds of worship.

ALABAMA

THE LEADER

Read Matthew 16:13-19.

"You are Peter, and on this rock I will build my church, and the gates of Hades will not overcome it" (v. 18).

A s a quarterback, he had no ability. As a leader, I've never had another like him." So spoke Bear Bryant about Pat Trammell.

Trammell was the Tide quarterback from 1959-61. He led the team in total offense in 1959 and in total scoring in 1960. He then had an All-American season that led the Tide to an undefeated season and the 1961 national championship. That season he set school records for total yards and passing yards.

All-American tackle Billy Neighbors called his teammate the "smartest and best football player [he] ever played with, period." He also said Trammell was the only guy he knew who could talk back to Coach Bryant and get away with it. "They'd send in a play and if Pat didn't want to run it, he wouldn't run it," Neighbors said. "You would hear them fussing at each other coming down the sideline. . . . But most of the time, Pat was right. He was a great, great football player."

Tackle Charlie Pell called him the "top dog of that football team." Pell recalled that a big tackle who played both ways always wanted to call timeout but Trammell would tell him to shut up and keep playing. "Everybody knew he could back it up, too."

Trammell kept his freshman rivals in line by charging into the room where some younger players were sitting, flipping a big switchblade into a tabletop, and asking if any of them were quarterbacks. Naturally, no one piped up. "Right then," said teammate Bill Oliver, "they all became halfbacks."

Dr. Pat Trammell remained a leader until the day he died at 28 of cancer. Asked in 1980 who his favorite player was, Bear Bryant replied, "Pat Trammel was the favorite *person* of my entire life."

Every aspect of life that involves people – every organization, every group, every project, every team -- must have a leader. If goals are to be reached, somebody must take charge.

Even the early Christian church was no different. Jesus knew this, so he designated the leader in Simon Peter, who was, in fact, quite an unlikely choice to assume such an awesome, world-changing responsibility. In *Twelve Ordinary Men*, John MacArthur described Simon as "ambivalent, vacillating, impulsive, unsub-missive." Hardly a man to inspire confidence in his leadership skills. Yet, Peter became, according to MacArthur, "the greatest preacher among the apostles" and the "dominant figure" in the birth of the church.

The implication for your own life is obvious and probably more than a little unsettling. You may think you lack the attri-butes necessary to make a good leader for Christ. But consider Simon Peter, an ordinary man who allowed Christ to rule his life and became the foundation upon which the Christian church was built.

He was a tremendous leader. Whatever it took, he would do it.
-- All-American Lee Roy Jordan on Pat Trammell

God's leaders are men and women
who allow Jesus to lead them.

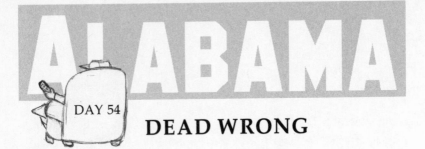

ALABAMA

DAY 54

DEAD WRONG

Read Matthew 26:14-16; 27:1-10.

"When Judas, who had betrayed him, saw that Jesus was condemned, he was seized with remorse" (v. 27:3).

Mark Ingram's winning the Heisman Trophy didn't just prove a whole bunch of so-called recruiting experts wrong. Turned out Bear Bryant was wrong, too.

It took 74 years for an Alabama player to win what has evolved into college football's highest individual prize. Of the top fourteen programs in terms of all-time wins, only Alabama had never had a Heisman winner.

Crimson Tide players have been finalists for the award eight times. Wide receiver and sometimes-quarterback David Palmer had finished the highest, third in 1993. Lee Roy Jordan, Johnny Musso, and Jay Barker all finished fourth. Harry Gilmer in 1945 and '47 and quarterbacks Pat Trammell in 1961 and Terry Davis in 1972 all finished fifth in the balloting. That was it.

Until Ingram came along and won the hardware that officially designated him as the best college football player in America.

Which must have gone down pretty hard with all those so-called recruiting experts. In high school in Flint, Mich., Ingram was at best a four-star prospect; usually, he drew three stars, which put him somewhere between the 50th and 75th running back in the country. He was "a good player, but nothing to write home about or build a team around." Not surprisingly, a lot of the big-time programs passed on him. Boy, were they all wrong.

After displaying flashes of brilliance as a freshman playing behind Glen Coffee, in 2009 Ingram emerged as the player around which the Tide built its team -- a national championship team. His Heisman Trophy laid to rest one of the school's persistent axioms: "At Alabama, our players don't win Heisman Trophies," Bryant once said. "Our teams win national championships."

Wrong -- at least for the Heisman Trophy part.

There's wrong, there's dead wrong, and there's Judas wrong. We've all been wrong in our lives, but we can at least honestly ease our conscience by telling ourselves we'll never be as wrong as Judas was. A close examination of Judas' actions, however, reveals that we can indeed replicate in our own lives the mistake Judas made that drove him to suicidal despair.

Judas ultimately regretted his betrayal of our Lord, but his sorrow and remorse, however boundless, could not save him. His attempt to undo his initial wrong was futile because he tried to fix everything himself rather than turning to God in repentance and begging for mercy.

While we can't literally betray Jesus to his enemies as Judas did, we can match Judas' failure in our own lives by not turning to God in Jesus' name and asking for forgiveness for our sins. In that case, we ultimately will be as dead wrong as Judas was.

The expectation level is high at the University of Alabama and it should be. What's wrong with people expecting excellence?
-- Gene Stallings

A sin is the first wrong; failing to ask God for forgiveness of it is the second.

DAY 55

HOME IMPROVEMENT

Read Ephesians 4:7-16.

"The body of Christ may be built up until we all reach unity in the faith and in the knowledge of the Son of God and become mature, attaining to the whole measure of the fullness of Christ" (vv. 12b, 13).

She was the greatest pitcher in the history of SEC softball to that time. And you're saying she needs improvement? That's exactly what Alabama softball coach Patrick Murphy determined after Shelley Laird completed her junior season in 2001.

Laird is an Alabama legend. From 1999-2002, she was twice All-America and four times All-SEC. She set virtually every school and many conference pitching records at the time. Among the Alabama career records she still holds are 115 wins, 39 shutouts, and 183 appearances. Her 38 wins as a sophomore in 2000 is still the Tide season record as are her 16 shutouts in 2001 and her 37 complete games in 2000. She struck out 18 batters, still the school record, in a game against Western Illinois.

As a junior in 2001, Laird won 32 games; her career earned run average at the time was 1.38. With 91 career wins, she started her senior season just three wins shy of becoming the winningest pitcher in SEC softball history.

And Murphy figured she had to become a better pitcher. That's because in a Tide loss to Michigan in the regional tournament in 2001, Murphy noticed that the Wolverine batters didn't offer at

CRIMSON TIDE

Laird's rise ball; instead, they patiently waited for a fast ball to hit. "They kind of knew she wasn't going to throw a change-up," Murphy said. So he decided Laird needed an off-speed pitch.

Work on the change-up began in the off-season. Laird even used her Christmas vacation to drag her father out into the backyard of their Texas home to serve as her catcher. With the addition of a new pitch, she won 24 more games in 2002 and led the Tide back to the regionals.

Just as Shelley Laird did, you try to improve at whatever you tackle. You attend training sessions and seminars to do your job better. You take golf or tennis lessons and practice to get better. You play that new video game until you master it. To get better at anything requires a dedication involving practice, training, study, and preparation.

Your faith life is no different. Jesus calls us to improve ourselves spiritually by becoming more mature in our faith. We can always know more about God's word, discover more ways to serve God, deepen our prayer life and our trust in God, and do a better job of being Jesus to other people through simple acts of kindness and caring. In other words, we can always become more like Jesus.

One day we will all stand before God as finished products. We certainly want to present him a mature dwelling, a spiritual mansion, not a hovel.

The principle is competing against yourself. It's about self-improvement, about being better than you were the day before.
-- Former NFL quarterback Steve Young

Spiritual improvement means a constant effort to become more like Jesus in our day-to-day lives.

DAY 56

THE NIGHTMARE

Read Mark 5:1-20.

"What do you want with me, Jesus, Son of the Most High God? Swear to God that you won't torture me!" (v. 7)

The whole business gave Bear Bryant nightmares and night sweats. He "sat up for hours at a time worrying about what this was doing to both his blood family and his football family."

"This" was the time after the *Saturday Evening Post* published a story on March 23, 1963, titled "The Story of a College Football Fix." The piece claimed the Bear and Wally Butts, Georgia's athletic director, had rigged the 1962 Alabama-Georgia game, which Alabama won 35-0.

That the *Post* would even publish such a story was bizarre to begin with. They relied on "the word of an Atlanta insurance man who claimed to have accidentally been cut in on a telephone conversation between Butts and Bryant." The man asserted that he heard Butts passing on inside information to Bryant.

This story came on the heels of another one published in October 1962 by the *Post* that accused Bryant of coaching a style of particularly brutal football. The story claimed that the Bear "wanted his players to hit first and think later." All-American defensive tackle Billy Neighbors said even the idea was absurd since Bryant taught smart football above everything else. "He never taught anything but tackling," Neighbors said. "And you better not get any penalties -- especially . . . if you took a cheap shot at somebody. He wouldn't play you if you did that."

Bryant once said that the *Post* "took 10 years of my life, and I billed them $10 million for it." Bryant's secretary, Linda Knowles, said the coach was "devastated that anyone would question his integrity."

Both Butts and Bryant won judgements against the *Post*, but in the interim, the whole sordid affair gave Bryant nightmares.

Falling. Drowning. Standing naked in a crowded room. Being unjustly accused. They're the stuff of nightmares, dreams that jolt us sweating and panting from our sleep in anxiety or downright terror. The film industry has used our common nightmares to create horror movies that allow us to experience our fears vicariously. This includes the formulaic "evil vs. good" movies in which demons and the like render good virtually helpless in the face of their power and ruthlessness.

The spiritual truth, though, is that it is evil that has come face to face with its worst nightmare: Jesus. We seem to understand that our basic mission as Jesus' followers is to further his kingdom and change the world through emulating him in the way we live and love others. But do we appreciate that in truly living for Jesus, we are daily tormenting the very devil himself?

Satan and his lackeys quake helplessly in fear before the power of almighty God that is in us through Jesus.

I can't have a nightmare tonight. I've just lived through one.
-- Darrell Imhoff, the opposing center the night Wilt Chamberlain
scored 100 points.

As the followers of Jesus Christ,
we are the stuff of Satan's nightmares.

DAY 57

DRY RUN

Read John 4:1-15.

*"Everyone who drinks this water will be thirsty again,
but whoever drinks the water I give him will never thirst.
Indeed, the water I give him will become in him a spring
of water welling up to eternal life" (vv. 13-14).*

The drought was of Biblical proportions; it lasted seven years. On Oct. 26, 2002, it ended not with a light spring shower but with a thunderstorm.

Since 1995, the Tide had endured what had become a "seven-year itch." Seven straight times Alabama had lost to the Tennessee. Volunteers. On this Saturday afternoon in Neyland Stadium, though, they said "good-bye to seven years of disappointment," waved "so long to fourth-quarter frustration," and touched off "a raucous celebration in the crimson-clad corner" of the stadium. They did it in convincing fashion, too, burying the 16th-ranked Vols 34-14.

"I told the team all week we were better than Tennessee," head coach Dennis Franchione said after the game. "I think they knew that but I didn't want any doubts in their mind."

From the first quarter on, no one had any doubts about which was the better team on this day. The Tide got off to a fast start when defensive back Gerald Dixon gathered in a ball UT laid on the turf and scampered 66 yards for a touchdown. An interception by safety Charles Jones in the end zone stopped a Vol

CRIMSON TIDE

drive, and the Tide marched 80 yards on six plays with Santonio Beard scoring from 10 yards out.

Bama led only 14-7 at the break, but the Tide blew the game open in the third quarter with a field goal by Kyle Robinson and a touchdown run by Tyler Watts. UT scored to make it 24-14, but they were through; the Tide wasn't.

Another Robinson field goal and a one-yard touchdown run from Beard completed the blowout and ended the drought.

You can walk across that river you boated on in the spring. The city's put all neighborhoods on water restriction, and that beautiful lawn you fertilized and seeded will turn a sickly, pale green and may lapse all the way to brown. Somebody wrote "Wash Me" on the rear window of your truck.

The sun bakes everything, including the concrete. The earth itself seems exhausted, just barely hanging on. It's a drought.

It's the way a soul looks that shuts God out.

God instilled thirst in us to warn us of our body's need for physical water. He also gave us a spiritual thirst that can be quenched only by his presence in our lives. Without God, we are like tumbleweeds, dried out and windblown, offering the illusion of life where there is only death.

Living water – water of life – is readily available in Jesus. We may drink our fill, and thus we slake our thirst and end our soul's drought – forever.

I have been here for four years and we kept saying next year is our year. It's finally happened.
                                        -- Charles Jones after the win over Tennessee

Our soul thirsts for God's refreshing presence.

ALABAMA

DAY 58

IMPRESSIONS

Read Mark 6:1-6.

"And [Jesus] was amazed at their lack of faith" (v. 6).

Antonio McDyess made quite an impression -- on his team-mates, his coach, the opposition, their coach, and on a national television audience. In short, he impressed everybody who saw him against the Penn Quakers in the opening round of the 1995 NCAA Tournament.

"I've never witnessed such domination," gushed teammate Jamal Faulkner. "That was a huge performance in a pressure-packed game," declared Tide coach David Hobbs.

McDyess' perfomance was indeed huge and it was indeed a pressure-packed game. The fifth-seeded Tide was favored over the 12th-seeded Quakers from the Ivy League, but nobody told the Penn guys and their five senior starters they weren't supposed to come out and whip 22-9 Alabama. The game was a thriller from start to overtime finish.

Penn led 38-37 at the break and took a lead heading into the last minutes. McDyess scored six straight points to force overtime and then hit the first four points to jumpstart an 11-0 Alabama run that apparently cinched the 91-85 win. Still, it took yet another play from McDyess to truly put the game away. Penn closed to within 88-85 before McDyess came up with a steal and went the length of the court for the dunk.

For the night, the 6-9 sophomore set a school record for the

NCAA Tournament with 39 points. That broke Leon Douglas' record of 35 points set against North Carolina in 1976. McDyess also had 19 rebounds, eight of them on the offensive end. He was 16 of 24 from the floor and 7 of 8 from the foul line.

"I'm not surprised," Hobbs said about McDyess' performance. Impressed -- but not surprised.

You bought that canary convertible mainly to impress the girls; a white Accord would transport you more efficiently. You seek out subtle but effective ways to gain the boss' approval. You may be all grown up now, but you still want your parents' favor. You dress professionally but strikingly and take your prospective clients to that overpriced steak house.

In our lives we are constantly seeking to impress someone else so they'll remember us and respond favorably to us. How often, though, do we pause to consider what impression we are making on Jesus with the way we live and the way we treat him? In God's scheme for salvation, it is only the good opinion of Jesus Christ that matters. On the day when we stand before God, our fate for eternity rests upon Jesus remembering and responding favorably to us.

We don't want to be like the folks in Jesus' hometown. Oh, they impressed him all right: with their lack of faith in him. This is not the impression we want to make.

I was certainly impressed with Antonio McDyess. He was awesome.
— Penn Coach Fran Dunphy

Jesus is the only one worth impressing,
and it is the depth of your faith – or the lack of it –
that impresses him.

DAY 59

IMPORTANT STUFF

Read Matthew 6:25-34.

*"Seek first his kingdom and his righteousness, and all
these things will be given to you as well" (v. 33).*

Marty Lyons was pretty much convinced his new head coach
had his priorities all out of line and that he had made a mistake
with his choice of schools.

When freshman Lyons sat in on his first meeting at Alabama
with Coach Bear Bryant in the summer of 1975, he couldn't believe
what he heard. The Bear said, "There are four things I want you
to do while you're here. Number one, always be proud of your
family. Number two, always be proud of your religion. Number
three, get an education. Number four, if we have time, let's try to
win some football games."

That meeting really confused Lyons, who sat there "scratching
my head wondering if I had chosen the right place, if the head
coach had his priorities in what I thought at the time were the
right order." What Lyons eventually learned, however, was that
he and not his head coach was the one whose priorities needed
some rearranging.

He spent his freshman year being convinced that the graduate
assistants were either trying to kill all the freshman or at least
run them all off. He spent his sophomore season seeing limited
playing time behind standout defensive tackle Bob Baumhower.

When he didn't letter, he challenged Bryant by telling him he was going to miss spring practice so he could play baseball. The Bear said that was fine with him, but "before you try to be good at two sports, try to be good at one." "That was the end of my baseball career," Lyons said.

And the beginning of gridiron greatness He was All-SEC in 1977, All-America in 1978, and a part of the famous goal-line stand in the 1979 Sugar Bowl. (See Devotion No. 2.) Along the way, he learned that if he kept his priorities in the order that Coach Bryant had listed them at that first meeting, then "good things happen."

Football may not be the most important thing in your life, but you do have priorities. What is it that you would surrender only with your dying breath? Your family? Every dime you have? Your Crimson Tide season tickets?

What about God? Would you denounce your faith in Jesus Christ rather than lose your children? Or everything you own?

God doesn't force us to make such unspeakable choices; nevertheless, followers of Jesus Christ often become confused about their priorities because so much in our lives clamors for attention and time. It all seems so worthwhile.

But Jesus' instructions are unequivocal: Seek God first. Turn to him first for help, fill your thoughts with what he wants for you and your life, use God's character as revealed in Jesus as the pattern for everything you do, and serve and obey him in all matters, at all moments.

God – and God alone – is No. 1.

I still try to keep those priorities [of Coach Bryant's] in mind.
                                        -- Marty Lyons when he was 47 years old

God should always be number one in our lives.

DAY 60

FOOD FOR THOUGHT

Read Genesis 9:1-7.

"Everything that lives and moves will be food for you. Just as I gave you the green plants, I now give you everything" (v. 3).

Before the biggest game of his life, one of Alabama's greatest players was not at all worried about the outcome or how he would play. He did have a concern, though: hot tamales.

Millard "Dixie" Howell was an All-American halfback in 1934. He was inducted into the College Football Hall of Fame in 1970. Each year the MVP of the annual spring A-Day game receives the Dixie Howell Award.

He played in an age when teams rarely passed the ball, but he teamed with All-American receiver Don Hutson "to make the forward pass a dangerous weapon." Legendary sportswriter Grantland Rice labeled him "The Human Howitzer." He was not just a passer as the left halfback in Coach Frank Thomas' Notre Dame box offense, but he also could run and kick.

On Jan. 1, 1935, the Tide won its fourth national title with a 29-13 win over Stanford in the Rose Bowl. Howell had the best game of his career, accounting for 239 offensive yards and 74 more on kick returns. Rice said Howell blasted Stanford "with one of the greatest all-around exhibitions football has ever known."

Football might have been on Howell's mind leading up to the Rose Bowl, but he was most concerned about hot tamales, for which he developed a craving on the trip to California. Tired of Thomas' strict dietary regime, Howell insisted that after the game he would eat six hot tamales, "win, lose or draw. I've been thinking about them so much out here that I've got to be dreaming about them. . . . The coach won't let us eat tamales now, but as soon as that game is over -- well, you watch."

Belly up to the buffet, boys and girls, for barbecue, sirloin steak, grilled chicken, and fried catfish with hush puppies and cheese grits (maybe even hot tamales). Rachael Ray's a household name; hamburger joints and pizza parlors, and taco stands lurk on every corner; and we have a TV channel devoted exclusively to food. We love our chow.

Food is one of God's really good ideas, but consider the complex divine plan that begins with a seed and ends with peas. The creator of all life devised a system in which living things are sustained and nourished physically through the sacrifice of other living things in a way similar to what Christ underwent to save us spiritually. Whether it's fast food or home-cooked, everything we eat is a gift from God secured through a divine plan in which some plants and animals have given up their lives.

Pausing to give thanks before we dive in seems the least we can do.

Last night, I dreamed about one hot tamale. It was as big as [Alabama tackle] Bill Lee.
-- Dixie Howell before the 1935 Rose Bowl

God created a system that nourishes us
through the sacrifice of other living things;
that's worth a thank-you.

DAY 61

A SURE THING

Read Romans 8:28-30.

"We know that in all things God works for the good of those who love him, who have been called according to his purpose" (v. 28).

The kick was a sure thing. Alabama's undefeated season, the national championship, maybe even the SEC title were all about to come crashing down.

The 2009 version of the Third Saturday in October was one of the most exciting games ever in the storied series. The game belonged to the defenses. Alabama used Leigh Tiffin's leg for a 9-3 halftime lead, and neither team could score in the third quarter.

Tiffin finished his perfect day with a 49-yard field goal to up the lead to 12-3 with only 6:31 left. The game looked like a sure thing, especially when Tennessee went three and out. The Vols downed the punt at the Bama four, but that didn't seem to matter, especially after Mark Ingram ripped off 13 yards for a first down and Tennessee was called for roughing the kicker.

Ingram was another sure thing. He hadn't fumbled all season, so the game was in the bag as the clock rolled on. But there it was; Ingram put the ball on the ground and Tennessee recovered.

The Vols covered 43 yards in eight plays to pull within 12-10 with 1:19 left to play. No problem; Alabama would recover the onside kick. But another sure thing went awry when Tennessee came up with the ball at their own 41.

CRIMSON TIDE

To the horror of the Crimson Nation, UT hit a third-down pass for 23 yards. The Vols set up shop at the Tide 27, well within field-goal range. A run set the ball up in the middle of the field, and a quarterback spike killed the clock with four seconds left.

"We just knew we were going to win," said Vol tight end Luke Stocker. But Terrence Cody didn't believe it was a sure thing at all. He crashed through, put his arm up, and slapped the kick away.

Football games aren't played on paper. That is, you attend an Alabama game expecting the Tide to win, but you don't know for sure. If you did, why bother to go? Any football game worth watching carries with it an element of uncertainty.

Life doesn't get played on paper either, which means that living, too, comes laden with uncertainty. You never know what's going to happen tomorrow or even an hour from now. Oh, sure, you think you know. For instance, right now you may be certain that you'll be at work Monday morning or that you'll have a job next month. Life's uncertainties, though, can intervene at any time and disrupt your nice, pat expectations.

One of the more fascinating aspects of a life lived in faith, how-ever, is that while you can't know for sure about this afternoon, you can know for certain about forever. Eternity is a sure thing because it's in God's hands. Your unwavering faith and God's sure promises lock in a certain future for you.

I just reached my arm up.
-- Terrence Cody on his block of the UT field goal

Life is unpredictable and tomorrow is uncertain;
only eternity is a sure thing
because God controls it.

ALIVE AGAIN

Read Matthew 28:1-10.

"He is not here; he has risen, just as he said. Come and see the place where he lay" (v. 6).

The 2005-06 season of Alabama's men's basketball team died on Jan. 7. Everybody knew it, even the head coach. And then resurrection came.

"It felt like a funeral." That was one reporter's observation in the aftermath of Alabama's 71-61 loss at home to "perennial cellar-dweller Ole Miss." The loss dropped a team that had hopes of making the NCAA Tournament for the fifth straight season to 7-6.

The news was much worse, though, than a demoralizing number of close losses. Against Ole Miss that night, the team lost senior leader Chuck Davis for the season to a knee injury. "Chuck's been the heart and soul for this particular team," said head coach Mark Gottfried. Even before Davis' injury the team lacked depth. After the injury, Gottfried typically rotated only seven players with point guard Ronald Steele and center Jermareo Davidson playing practically every minute. In an overtime win over Vanderbilt, they played all 45 minutes.

So the Tide was dead and buried. Rest in peace. Only "a long, painful season remained."

After the game, a disheartened Gottfried refused to give up. He said his guys wanted a berth in the NCAA Tournament, and

CRIMSON TIDE

"We've got to find a way to get there." In other words, they had to resurrect the dead season.

Which is exactly what they did. The team promptly surprised everybody by winning six of their next eight. Before the season and the SEC tournament ended, the Tide was 17-12.

On Sunday, March 12, the team gathered around a TV set and anxiously watched the announcing of the tournament brackets. They were in; they had resurrected the season.

All of this language of resurrection is figurative, of course. No one on the 2005-06 Alabama team actually pulled a gun and shot the season to death. We often speak figuratively of resurrected careers and seasons in sports. A team is given up for dead until it comes alive and wins a game.

While literal resurrections occur in the New Testament, one in particular stands alone. All others are merely the postponement of death -- perhaps more correctly termed "resuscitations" -- but when Jesus walked out of that tomb on the first Easter morning, he threw off not only his burial cloths but death itself. On that day, God created something new: the resurrection life that one day will be the only one.

That's because resurrection is a fact of life for the followers of Jesus. When Christ left that tomb behind, he also left death behind for all who believe that he is indeed the savior of the world.

If I sat up here and said [making the NCAA Tournament's] an unrealistic goal, that would be unfair to our guys.
-- Mark Gottfried after the Jan. 7 loss to Ole Miss

Jesus' resurrection forever ended death's hold on life; life has won.

DAY 63

TEARS IN HEAVEN

Read Revelation 21:1-8.

"[God] will wipe every tear from their eyes. There will be no more death or mourning or crying or pain" (v. 4).

It's the first time I've cried in twenty or thirty years," declared Bear Bryant. "And believe me, I really did."

In 1965, a writer told a friend that he had walked into Bryant's hotel room and overheard the words written above. He agreed Bryant did indeed look all choked up. "What's wrong with Paul?" he asked. "He just lost an assistant coach," the man replied. "How old was he?" the writer asked. "Twenty-nine." "That's awfully young!" the writer exclaimed. "How did he die?" "Oh, he didn't die," his friend assured him. "He just went to Texas A&M."

The coach that Bryant lost was Gene Stallings, one of those legendary thirty-five "Junction Boys" who made it through the grueling pre-season boot camp of Bryant's first year as A&M's head coach. After Stallings graduated, he stayed on as an assistant coach. When Bryant moved to Alabama, Stallings came with him. Then when A&M called in 1965, Stallings returned to College Station to serve as head football coach and athletic director. That's when Bryant's rare tears came.

Nobody was crying in Tuscaloosa, however, when Stallings came "home" in 1990. Eli Gold wrote, "He was coming not a minute too soon." He came back after the decade of the 1980s during which the program "weather[ed] some serious ups and downs" in the wake of Bryant's retirement in 1982. In his seven seasons at the helm, Stallings led the Tide to a 70-16-1 record. They won the SEC West Division title four times and at one stretch won twenty-eight straight games.

The apex of Stallings' time at Alabama came in 1992 when the Tide went undefeated and won the national championship. The tears of joy were flowing again in Tuscaloosa.

When your parents died. When a friend told you she was divorcing. When you broke your collarbone. When you watch a sad movie. You cry. Crying is as much a part of life as are breathing and indigestion. Usually our tears are brought on by pain, sorrow, or disappointment.

But what about when your children were born? When you discovered Jesus Christ? When Alabama beats Auburn? Those times elicit tears too; we cry at the times of our greatest, most overwhelming joy.

Thus, while there will be tears in Heaven, they will only be tears of sheer, unmitigated, undiluted joy. The greatest joy possible, a joy beyond our imagining, must occur when we finally see Christ. If we shed tears when Alabama wins a game, can we really believe that we will stand dry-eyed and calm in the presence of Jesus?

What we will not shed in Heaven are tears of sorrow and pain.

I cried because I'm so proud one of my little Junction Boys is going back there to take over. Secondly, I cried because I'm upset about losing him.
-- Bear Bryant on losing Gene Stallings to Texas A&M

Tears in Heaven will be like everything else there:
a part of the joy we will experience.

ALABAMA

THE ANSWER

Read Colossians 2:2-10.

"My purpose is that they . . . may know the mystery of God, namely, Christ, in whom are hidden all the treasures of wisdom and knowledge" (vv. 2, 3).

Jeremiah Castille was a self-admitted "bad kid" heading down the wrong road until he found the answers on a summer night right there in his neighborhood.

Louis Campbell, Alabama's secondary coach from 1980-84, said Castille "had a lot of physical, God-given talent" but what made him even more special was that "you knew right from the start that he had a spiritual basis in his life."

That wasn't the way it started out for Jeremiah as a boy in Phenix City. He called his family "dysfunctional. I had a mom and a dad, but I grew up in an alcoholic family" and "around domestic violence. My mom and dad fought multiple times." Looking back on his youth, Castille understands that his home life is the kind "most people don't make it out of." They become "a victim of their environment."

Castille was certainly headed that way. Before he was out of junior high, he had been both suspended and expelled for fighting. "I was a bad kid, and I was just doing what I had learned at home," he said.

So what happened? The summer after he was expelled, he attended a revival just down the street from his home. "The Lord saved me that summer, and I committed to a personal relationship with Jesus Christ." He had found the answer.

Castille went on to be a three-year starter at defensive back for Alabama, setting the school record at the time with 16 career interceptions. He was All-America in 1982 and served as a pallbearer at Bear Bryant's funeral. Today, still true to the answer he found that crucial summer night, he heads his own ministry.

Experience is essentially the uncovering of answers to some of life's questions, both trivial and profound. You often discover to your dismay that as soon as you learn a few answers, the questions change. Your children get older, your health worsens, your financial situation changes -- these new circumstances all present questions that require a new set of answers.

No answers, though, are more important than those you seek in your search for God and the meaning of life because they determine your fate for all eternity. Since a life of faith is a journey and not a destination, the questions do indeed change with your circumstances. The "why" or the "what" you ask God when you're a teenager is vastly different from the quandaries you ponder as an adult. No matter how you phrase the question, though, the answer inevitably centers on Jesus. And that answer never changes.

When you're a driver and you're struggling in the car, you're looking for God to come out of the sky and give you a magical answer.
-- NASCAR's Rusty Wallace

It doesn't matter what the question is;
if it has to do with life, temporal or eternal,
the answer lies in Jesus.

SHAPE UP

Read Luke 12:35-40.

"You also must be ready, because the Son of Man will come at an hour when you do not expect him" (v. 40).

They kept playing. And playing. And playing. And -- one more time -- playing. When it was finally over long past the point of exhaustion for both the players and the fans, Alabama and Duke had played the longest game in NCAA women's basketball play-off history.

On March 18, 1995, the Tide defeated Duke 121-120 in the second round of the NCAA Tournament. The game needed four overtimes to decide a winner. Despite her disappointment in the loss, Duke head coach Gail Goestenkors called the contest, "the best game I've ever witnessed."

The hero of the game for Alabama clearly was All-American guard Niesa Johnson, who re-entered the game with four fouls with 8:37 to go in the second half and never fouled out. She hit a 3-point shot with only 1.6 seconds left in regulation to tie the game at 81 and get the overtime parade started. Duke apparently had the game sewed up with a three-point lead and the ball until Marlene Stevenson took a charge with 13:8 seconds left.

With 2.2 seconds left in the first overtime, Johnson hit two free throws to tie the game at 89. The moment wasn't without its anxiety for Tide fans as one of her shots clanked around on the rim before deciding to drop through.

CRIMSON TIDE

And so it went until finally, with 7.8 seconds left in the fourth overtime, Johnson hit a pair of free throws to give the Tide a four-point lead that held up. After 60 minutes of exhausting basketball, the 22-8 Tide was on its way to the Sweet Sixteen. Johnson finished with 28 points, 12 rebounds, and 14 assists.

"I've never been involved in a game of this magnitude," Tide coach Rick Moody said. Or -- he added -- one of this length.

Like a basketball game with a number of overtimes, life is an endurance sport; you're in it for the long haul. So you schedule a physical, check your blood pressure for free at the supermarket pharmacy, walk or jog, and hop on the treadmill that hides under the bed or doubles as a coat rack.

The length of your life, however, is really the short haul when compared to the long haul that is eternity. To prepare yourself for eternity requires conditioning that is spiritual rather than physical. Jesus prescribed a regimen so his followers could be in tip-top spiritual shape. It involves not just occasional exercise but a way of living every day that involves abiding faith, decency, witnessing, mercy, trust, and generosity.

If Crimson Tide basketball players aren't ready when the first whistle blows, they will lose a game when the last whistle sounds. If you aren't ready when Jesus calls, you lose eternity.

Proper conditioning is that fleeting moment between getting ready and going stale.
-- Legendary Alabama Football Coach Frank Thomas

Physical conditioning is good for the short run,
but you also need to be in peak spiritual shape
for the long haul.

DAY 66

RAIN CHECK

Read Genesis 9:8-17.

*"I establish my covenant with you: Never again will all
life be cut off by the waters of a flood; never again will
there be a flood to destroy the earth" (v. 11).*

Sally Stabler was cold and wet, shivering in her drenched
clothes. She had forgotten her umbrella and her raincoat, and
so she sat there "drowning for three quarters in the rain storm
that came spilling out of the Great Smoky Mountains 45 minutes
before kickoff."

But no way was she going to leave; her son was on the field.
In fact, "nobody among the 56,368 people in there bumping
umbrellas [was] budging." After all, this was Alabama-Tennessee
and this was a thriller, rain or no rain. On the Third Saturday in
October, 1966, the Tide struggled to hold its undefeated season
together. Tennessee led 10-8 as time and the rain ran on.

With only nine minutes left to play and the ball at the Tide
25, Mrs. Stabler's boy, Kenny, trotted onto the field and urged his
team to stay calm. On third and four, Stabler hit running back Les
Kelley to the Bama 45. Split end Ray Perkins hauled in a pass for
20 more yards to the Volunteer 35. Gene Raburn got nine on a pair
of runs; Stabler kept it and got outside for 11 to the UT 15.

The Tide then got a mammoth break on this day of wet and
slippery footballs. On second down from the 12, the ball popped
out of Kelley's hands, hit the turf, and bounced once right into

Perkins' mitts. Tennessee refused to budge after that, setting up a field-goal attempt that was usually a chip shot, but not on this day. Sure enough, the snap was low and Stabler had trouble grasping the wet ball. Both his hands were still on it when Steve Davis hit it "a yard or two inside the left upright."

11-10 Alabama and that's the way it ended. The weather sure got a lot better for the Tide faithful.

The kids are on go for their picnic. Your golf game is set. You have rib eyes and smoked sausage ready for the grill when the gang comes over tonight. And then it rains.

Sometimes you can slog on through a downpour as Alabama and Tennessee and their fans did that October back in 1966. Often, however, the rain simply washes away your carefully laid plans, and you can't do anything about it.

Rain falls when and where it wants to without checking with you. It answers only to God, the one who controls the heavens from which it comes, the ground on which it falls, and everything in between -- territory that should include you.

While God has absolute dominance over the rain and all other variations of the weather, interestingly enough, he will take control of your life only if you let him. In daily seeking his will for your life, you discover that you can live so as to be walking in the sunshine even when it's raining.

Don't pray when it rains if you don't pray when the sun shines.
-- Pitcher and Philosopher Leroy "Satchel" Paige

Into each life some rain must fall,
but you can live in the glorious light
of God's love even during a downpour.

DAY 67

GOD'S CONQUERORS

Read John 16:19-33.

"In this world you will have trouble. But take heart! I have overcome the world" (v. 33b).

Two blocked kicks, three turnovers, a spate of penalties, a wild dog, and an inflatable Elvis. The Tide overcame them all to win the 1995 Citrus Bowl.

On Jan. 2, Alabama defeated Ohio State 24-17 with a surprising offensive show that rolled up a season-high 521 yards. Senior quarterback Jay Barker completed 18 of 37 passes for 317 yards and no interceptions. Game MVP Sherman Williams set an Alabama bowl record with 166 yards rushing. He scored two touchdowns and accounted for 359 yards with his rushing, receiving, and kickoff returns.

All of this sounds like the Tide pulled off the win like a well-oiled machine. The game was, in fact, pretty much a mess with sluggish play, penalties, blocked kicks, and fumbles. A dog ran onto the field and delayed the game for five minutes, giving quite a good chase to some harried security guards. A 30-foot inflatable Elvis used for the halftime extravaganza likewise refused to leave the field. The second-half kickoff was delayed while the hunk of burning love was deflated.

Late in the game, the Tide had one more obstacle to overcome: a 17-14 Ohio State lead. At this point, the game suddenly turned crisp. Michael Proctor's field goal with 4:27 left tied the game.

CRIMSON TIDE

Then Williams took a short Barker pass and turned it into a game-winning 50-yard touchdown with only 42 seconds left.

When cornerback Tommy Johnson spiked a Buckeye pass to the turf of the end zone on the game's last play, the Tide had overcome the opposition, its own mistakes, Elvis, and the dog to do what Alabama does best: win.

We each have a choice to make about how we live. We can merely survive, passing each day hoping that everything doesn't get any worse, or we can overcome as the Crimson Tide does.

We often hear inspiring stories of people who triumph by overcoming especially daunting obstacles. Those barriers may be physical or mental disabilities or great personal tragedies or injustice. When we hear of them, we may well respond with a little prayer of thanksgiving that life has been kinder to us.

But all people of faith, no matter how drastic the obstacles they face, must ultimately overcome the same opponent: the Satan-infested world. Some do have it tougher than others, but we all must fight daily to remain confident and optimistic.

Merely to survive from day to day is to give up by surrendering our trust in God's involvement in our daily life. To overcome, however, is to stand up to the world and fight its temptations that would erode the armor of our faith in Jesus Christ.

Today is a day to overcome by remaining faithful. The very hosts of Heaven wait to hail the conquering hero.

A good team finds a way to win games, and that's what Alabama did.
-- Ohio State Coach John Cooper after the Citrus Bowl

**Life's difficulties provide us a chance
to experience the true joy of victory in Jesus.**

DAY 68

NAME CALLING

Read Exodus 3:13-20.

"God said to Moses, 'I AM WHO I AM. This is what you are to say to the Israelites: 'I AM has sent me to you'' (v. 14).*

The running back Bear Bryant said was the finest he ever coached had a nickname that embarrassed him no end.

From 1969-71, halfback Johnny Musso bulled his way to a Tide-record 2,741 yards (subsequently eclipsed by Shaun Alexander, Bobby Humphrey and Kenneth Darby). He was All-America in 1970 and was voted to Alabama's Team of the Century.

Before Musso's sophomore season, Alabama sports information director Charley Thornton decided that Musso needed a flashy nickname for publicity. So he went to Musso and asked him what his nickname was. "Johnny" came the somewhat less-than-inspired reply. As Musso described the process, Thornton "tried several things and they went from bad to worse" during the summer. "They were all bad, but the one I really remember was Johnny 'GoGo' Musso."

Musso thought Thornton had given up by the time the 1969 season opened against Virginia Tech in Blacksburg. But when he showed up for the pregame meal, "people immediately started laughing at me and making horse noises." Sometime tossed a local paper his way with its headline: "Alabama to Unleash the Italian Stallion." From then on, the name stuck.

CRIMSON TIDE

Musso later played Canadian football with a linebacker named Carl Weathers, who teased him about his awful nickname. Weathers, of course, played Apollo Creed in the *Rocky* movies, which featured Rocky Balboa, aka the "Italian Stallion." Musso always wondered if his own nickname had been the inspiration.

Nicknames such as Johnny Musso's the "Italian Stallion" are usually not slapped haphazardly upon individuals but rather reflect widely held perceptions about the person named. Proper names do that also.

Nowhere throughout history, however, has this concept been more prevalent that in the Bible, where a name is not a mere label but is an expression of the essential nature of the named one. That is, a person's name reveals his or her character. Even God shares this concept; to know the name of God is to know God as he has chosen to reveal himself to us.

We don't put that much stock in the name we select for our newborns these days, but over the course of a lifetime, our name does achieve a significance of its own. That is, our reputation -- our very name -- precedes us. The mere mention of our name evokes positive and/or negative associations and reactions from those who hear it. What our name signifies to others depends upon the type of person we are.

Our name does the same thing in Heaven at the very throne of God, who, after all, knows each of us by name.

The nickname really embarrassed me for a long time.
-- Johnny Musso on being dubbed the "Italian Stallion"

**No name is more important than being called
a child of God because you know Jesus.**

DAY 69

UNBELIEVABLE

Read Hebrews 3:7-19.

"See to it, brothers, that none of you has a sinful, unbelieving heart that turns away from the living God" (v. 12).

During the 1955 season, Alabama's George Linn made one of the most unbelievable shots in basketball history.

At the time, Linn was a 6-4 junior forward who came South from Columbus, Ohio, with Coach Johnny Dee in 1953. An All-America in 1956, Linn scored 1,444 points in his career, a total that was second then only to teammate Jerry Harper. His career average of 22.2 points per game is still the fifth-best in Tide history.

Against South Carolina on Jan. 4, 1955, Linn made what was called "the unofficial longest field goal in college history." The Tide were on their way to a 77-55 romp past Frank McGuire's North Carolina Tar Heels in old Foster Auditorium. As the first half was about to end, Linn rebounded a missed shot, turned, and launched the ball 84 feet, 11 inches. Unbelievably, the ball found the net for a basket.

Harper never forgot the unbelievable play. "When it went in the place sure got quiet," he recalled. "You could hear a pin drop for the longest time. Then it sure enough broke loose." Teammate Leon Marlaire said the shot was like throwing a touchdown pass. "It hit squarely on the board and dropped squarely through the goal. It never touched the rim."

CRIMSON TIDE

McGuire got on his hands and knees on the court and marked the spot, declaring it the longest shot ever. A metal marker was inserted into the floor to commemorate Linn's legendary heave.

Unfortunately, no visual record remains of Alabama's most unbelievable shot ever because the athletic department at the time filmed only SEC games at home.

What we claim not to believe in reveals much about us. UFOs. Global warming. Sasquatch. Aluminum baseball bats and the designated hitter.

Most of what passes for our unbelief has little effect on our lives. Does it matter much that we don't believe a Ginsu knife can stay sharp after repeatedly slicing through tin cans? Or that any other team besides Alabama is worth pulling for?

That's not the case, however, when Jesus and God are part of the mix. Quite unbelievably, we often hear people blithely assert they don't believe in God. Or brazenly declare they believe in God but don't believe Jesus was anything but a good man and a great teacher.

At this point, unbelief becomes dangerous because God doesn't fool around with scoffers. He locks them out of the Promised Land, which isn't a country in the Middle East but Heaven itself.

Given that scenario, it's downright unbelievable that anyone would not believe.

Football is an incredible game. Sometimes it's so incredible, it's unbelievable.

-- Tom Landry

Perhaps nothing is as unbelievable as that some people insist on not believing in God or his son.

DAY 70

THE SIMPLE LIFE

Read 1 John 1:5-10.

"If we confess our sins, he is faithful and just and will forgive us our sins and purify us from all unrighteousness" (v. 9).

When the Tide opened the 2008 season with a surprising blowout of highly regarded Clemson, the winning formula was a very simple one that harkened back to the days of the Bear.

"If we're going to win this game," Coach Nick Saban said before the Sept. 6 kickoff in the Georgia Dome, "our defensive line is going to have to whip their offensive line." With that simple formula before them, Alabama went out and smashed the 9th-ranked Tigers 34-10. "We got whipped about every way you can get whipped," lamented Clemson Coach Tommy Bowden.

The key whipping, though, took place up front just as Saban wanted. The Alabama players went into the game with their ears ringing from all the pre-season publicity and hype heaped on the Tigers' tailback tandem of James Davis and C.J. Spiller. Stop these two -- and the Tide could control the game and the outcome.

"Doesn't matter how good they are if they got no hole to go through," noted Tide linebacker Brandon Fanney. What Alabama unleashed on the helpless Tigers was a physical, swarming defense that totally whipped the Tigers' offensive line.

Shutting down the Tigers' rushing attack meant Clemson's offense was on the field for only 18:47 all night long. Fumble, punt, field goal, punt, interception, 70 total yards: That's what Clemson did in the first half.

The simple formula of winning at the line kept on working in the last half. Clemson's only points came on a kickoff return. The Tigers wound up with zero yards rushing for the game.

Perhaps the simple life in America was doomed by the arrival of the programmable VCR, itself rendered defunct by more sophisticated technology. Since then, we've been on what seems to be an inevitably downward spiral into ever more complicated lives. Even windshield wipers have multiple settings, and operating a clothes dryer now requires a graduate degree.

But we might do well in our own lives to mimic the simple formula Nick Saban used to overpower Clemson. That is, we should approach our lives with the keen awareness that success requires simplicity, a sticking to the basics: Revere God, love our families, honor our country, do our best.

Theologians may make what God did in Jesus as complicated as quantum mechanics and the infield fly rule, but God kept it simple for us: believe, trust, and obey. Believe in Jesus as the Son of God, trust that through him God makes possible our deliverance from our sins into Heaven, and obey God in the way he wants us to live. It's simple, but it's the true winning formula, the way to win for all eternity.

I think God made it simple. Just accept Him and believe.
-- Bobby Bowden

Life continues to get ever more complicated,
but God made it simple for us
when he showed up as Jesus.

DAY 71

AS A RULE

Read Luke 5:27-32.

"Why do you eat and drink with tax collectors and 'sinners'?" (v. 30b)

One of the most unusual rules in college football history once led indirectly to an Alabama touchdown in the Rose Bowl.

Alabama wide receiver Don Hutson had as much influence on football as anyone who ever played. Hutson wore the Crimson and White from 1932-34; an All-America in 1934, he was so good that he still holds several NFL pass reception records. "Hutson is credited with inventing modern pass receiving" and with creating many of the routes receivers still run. He forever changed the way both college and pro football teams used the forward pass. Coach Frank Thomas called him "the best player I ever coached."

His last game was the 1935 Rose Bowl against Stanford for the national championship. Stanford scored first and the Tide really got a scare when halfback Dixie Howell (See Devotion No. 60.) came down with stomach cramps. Howell was the throwing end of Hutson's receptions, so Thomas decided to forgo the passing game in favor of the run until Howell recovered. He sent Hutson into the game with instructions for a set of running plays.

A bizarre rule prohibited a sub coming into the game from speaking in the huddle until after the first play was over. So Joe Riley, Howell's replacement, quite naturally figured that Hutson's presence meant Thomas wanted a pass play. Totally against his

CRIMSON TIDE

coach's wishes, Riley let fly with a 50-yard bomb that Hutson caught on the Stanford 14 and ran in for a touchdown.

After that, Thomas went with the passing game, Hutson finished with six catches for 165 yards and two touchdowns, and Alabama won 29-13.

As football players do, you live by rules others set up. Some lender determined the interest rate on your mortgage and your car loan. You work hours and shifts somebody else established. Someone else decided what day your garbage gets picked up and what school district your house is in.

Jesus encountered societal rules also, including a strict set of religious edicts that dictated what company he should keep, what people, in other words, were fit for him to socialize with, talk to, or share a meal with. Jesus ignored the rules, choosing love instead of mindless obedience and demonstrating his disdain for society's rules by mingling with the outcasts, the lowlifes, the poor, and the misfits. Jesus' attitude toward the rules and those who set them ultimately got him killed.

Just as did Jesus' society, contemporary America has its own arbitrary rules about who is or is not desirable. Jesus thus mandates that his followers challenge those rules in his name and the name of the love he preached and modeled. Every day, we must choose: the rules or Jesus.

You have three rules to win as a coach: Surround yourself with people who love football, recognize winners, and have a plan for everything.
-- Bear Bryant

No matter what the rules say, for the follower of Jesus, no one is undesirable or beyond caring for.

DAY 72

HAVE YOU HEARD?

Read Mark 1:21-28.

"News about him spread quickly over the whole region"
(v. 28).

On Oct. 4, 1969, ABC took what was then regarded as a huge risk: It put college football on prime-time TV. What it got for its gamble was one of the greatest college games ever.

Alabama and Ole Miss were ready to go at Legion Field, but they had to wait around a while, thanks to Lawrence Welk. The bandleader's contract didn't allow the network to preempt him, so everyone had to wait until after 8 p.m. to witness history.

The game was expected to be a defensive slugfest despite the presence of Archie Manning. At halftime, "the suits at ABC were nervous" as the score was a pedestrian 14-7. But the game heated up so much that the audience increased as the last half wore on.

For the night, Manning was unstoppable. He set NCAA records for passing yards (436), pass attempts (52), completions (39), and total offense (539 yards) and accounted for four touchdowns. "He was Superman that night," Tide QB Scott Hunter said. But Hunter also had a record-breaking night, setting an Alabama standard with 300 yards passing.

Midway through the fourth quarter, Hunter gave Bama a 27-26 lead with a quarterback sneak. Manning struck again, though, and Hunter had to lead the Tide back down the field. With less than four minutes left, Alabama faced fourth and long at the

CRIMSON TIDE

Rebel 14. Ole Miss blitzed, and Johnny Musso's block gave Hunter enough time before he was buried. His pass hit receiver George Ranager at the 5. He broke a tackle and scored. Alabama won 33-32.

Had the game been ordinary, prime-time college football might have been one-and-done for a while, but never again would the game have to wait for Lawrence Welk. The word was out.

Commercials and advertisements for products and services inundate us. Turn on your computer: ads pop up without any prompting from you. Watch NASCAR: decals cover the cars and the drivers' uniforms. TV, radio, newspapers, billboards -- everyone's trying to get the word out the best way possible.

Jesus was no different in that he used the most effective and efficient means of advertising he had at his disposal to spread his message of salvation and hope among the masses. That was word of mouth. In his ministry, Jesus didn't isolate himself; instead, he moved from town to town among the common people, preaching, teaching, and healing. Those who encountered Jesus then told others about their experience, thus spreading the word about the good news.

Almost two millennia later, nothing's really changed. Speaking to someone else about Jesus remains the best way to get the word out, and the best advertisement of all is a changed life.

It became an iconic game because it established college football as legitimate, prime-time entertainment.

-- *Mike Aresco, CBS Sports*

**The best advertising for Jesus is word of mouth,
telling others what he has done for you.**

DAY 73

LOST AND FOUND

Read Luke 15:11-32.

"This brother of yours was dead and is alive again; he was lost and is found" (v. 32).

Michael Thompson lost his home, his car, and his golf scholarship. Out of it all, he found a better life.

Thompson earned All-Conference USA honors and won four tournaments in his first two seasons on the golf team at Tulane University. He was quite content as his junior season of 2005-06 approached. Then virtually overnight he lost everything about his life as he knew it – thanks to Hurricane Katrina.

Thompson evacuated his New Orleans apartment, figuring he would be gone for a few days at most. Before he left town with his roommate to wait out the storm in Houston, he dropped his car off at a local body shop. He even planned to get in a little golf while he was away.

Of course, the mini-vacation turned into a major tragedy. Thompson and his roommate had to finish the semester at SMU. His roommate's father drove to New Orleans to retrieve their belongings from the apartment. Since it was on the second floor, their personal effects were undamaged. Thompson never did see his car again, though.

His life continued to change when Tulane decided to drop golf in the wake of the disaster. Thompson had lost his college scholarship and had to start the recruiting process all over again.

CRIMSON TIDE

He wound up at Alabama, and everything he lost was clearly the Tide's gain. As a first-team All-America in 2008, he won the SEC individual title in leading the Tide to their first SEC championship in 29 years.

"It's been a wild ride," Thompson said about the old life he lost and the new one he found.

From car keys to friendships, fortunes to reading glasses, loss is a feature of the unfolding panorama of our lives. We win some, we lose some; that's life.

Loss has varying degrees of meaning for us as it may range from the devastatingly tragic to the momentarily annoying. No loss, however, is as permanently catastrophic as the loss of our very souls.

While "being lost" is one of Christianity's many complex symbols, the concept is simple: The lost are those who have chosen to separate themselves from God, to live without an awareness of God in an unrepentant lifestyle contrary to his commandments and tenets. Being lost is a state of mind as much as a way of life.

It's a one-sided decision, though, since God never leaves the lost; they leave him. No one is a born loser, and neither does anyone have to remain lost. All it takes is a turning back to God; all it takes is a falling into the open arms of Jesus Christ, the good shepherd.

It's just a blessing that it worked out this way for me.
-- Michael Thompson

From God's point of view, we are all either lost or found; interestingly, we – not God – determine into which group we land.

ALABAMA

DAY 74

BEST FRIENDS

Read Ecclesiastes 4:9-12.

"If one falls down, his friend can help him up. But pity the man who falls and has no one to help him up!" (v. 10)

Because Kevin Jackson had a friend, Alabama kept an All-American safety.

In September 1995, Jackson was ready to quit the Alabama football team and leave school. He had even met with the Samford football coaches to discuss transferring and eligibility.

Jackson's decision had not come suddenly. A move in 1995 from linebacker, where he had always played, to strong safety had not set well with him. Then in the third game of the '95 season, Arkansas upset Alabama, and Jackson could only watch. He had been benched the week before.

"I was going to transfer, no doubt about it," he said. "I wasn't going to give up football. I just felt I wasn't needed [at Alabama]." So what happened? Darrell Blackburn did.

Blackburn was Jackson's roommate and a Tide linebacker. Most of all, he was Jackson's friend, and he saw what was going on. When Jackson tried to leave Bryant Hall, Blackburn stopped him. "He told me I wasn't going to leave," Jackson recalled. "'I'm taking the keys to your car,' he said. 'You're not quitting.' We sat down in our dorm room and talked for a long time." Blackburn told his friend to stick it out, that his turn would come.

And indeed it did. Jackson led the team with five interceptions that season, including three in a 31-0 romp over Georgia, after which *Sports Illustrated* named him the national Player of the Week. In an All-American senior season, Jackson had seven interceptions.

But his friend wasn't on the field with him. Darrell Blackburn, who led the Tide in sacks in 1995, had to give up football before the '96 season began because of a degenerative kidney.

Lend her your car or some money. Comfort him when he's down. Talk him out of a bad decision like quitting a football team. What wouldn't you do for a good friend?

We are wired for friendship. Our psyche drives us to seek both the superficial company of others that casual acquaintance provides and the more meaningful intimacy that true friendship furnishes. We are perhaps at our noblest when we selflessly help a friend.

So if we wouldn't think of turning our back on our friends, why would we not be the truest, most faithful friend of all by sharing with them the gospel of Jesus Christ? Without hesitating or even thinking about it, we give a friend a ride. On the other hand, we know someone for years and don't do what we can to save her from eternal damnation. Apparently, we are quite willing to spend all of eternity separated from our friends.

What kind of lousy friend is that?

I don't think he could live without me. I know I couldn't live without him.

— *Kevin Jackson on his friend, Darrell Blackburn*

**A true friend introduces a friend
to his friend Jesus.**

ALABAMA

DAY 75

REVELATION

Read Isaiah 53.

*"But he was pierced for our transgressions, he was
crushed for our iniquities; the punishment that brought us
peace was upon him, and by his wounds we are healed"
(v. 5).*

In 1961 it became official. Bear Bryant was a prophet."

All-American Tackle Billy Neighbors was a freshman in 1958
when Bear Bryant took over the moribund Alabama football
program. He was present when Bryant first met with his new
team, and he could not believe what he heard. "He told us [that]
in four years, if we believed in his plan and dedicated ourselves
to being the best we could be, we would be national champions."
And what was Neighbors' reaction? "I thought he was crazy."

With good reason. Alabama had won only four games in the
last three years. But 1958 was a turnaround year, a start on the
long road back. A 5-4-1 record doesn't sound like much, but the
fives wins were more than the total of the previous three seasons.
Then came a 7-2-2 record in 1959 that included a 10-0 win over
Auburn and a bowl game. In 1960, the Tide went 8-1-2 and tied
Texas in the Bluebonnet Bowl.

And so in 1961 all those freshmen – the Bear's first players
– were seniors. Their names are legendary now among the
Crimson Nation: All-Americans Neighbors, Pat Trammell, and
Lee Roy Jordan; Darwin Holt, Mike Fracchia (All-SEC), Butch

CRIMSON TIDE

Wilson, Billy Battle, Bill Oliver, and Tommy Brooker. They went 11-0 and won the national championship. No one even came close as the defense allowed only 25 points all season. They blasted the Vols 34-3, after which an excited Bryant promised them all a ring because of the win.

They whipped Arkansas 10-3 in the Sugar Bowl, and Bear Bryant the prophet was the national coach-of-the-year.

In our jaded age, we have relegated prophecy to dark rooms where mysterious women gather suckers around a table and peer into a crystal ball or clasp our sweaty palms while uttering vague generalities. At best, we understand a prophet as someone who predicts future events as Bear Bryant did with his 1961 national title.

When we open the pages of the Bible, though, we encounter something radically different. A prophet is a messenger from God, one who relays divine revelation to others.

Prophets seem somewhat foreign to us because in one very real sense the age of prophecy is over. In the name of Jesus, we have access to God through our prayers and through scripture. In searching for God's will for our lives, we seek divine revelation. We may speak only for ourselves and not for the greater body of Christ, but we do not need a prophet to discern what God would have us do. We need faith in the one whose birth, life, and death fulfilled more than 300 Bible prophecies.

You can't look at a rabbit and see how fast he can run.
-- Bear Bryant when asked if his 1961 team looked like a winner

**Persons of faith continuously seek
a word from God for their lives.**

A CHANGE OF PLANS

Read Genesis 18:20-33.

"The Lord said, 'If I find fifty righteous people in the city of Sodom, I will spare the whole place for their sake'" (v. 26).

Ozzie Newsome had already decided he wasn't going to play any more football. Alabama fans are still grateful that he had a change of plans.

Newsome is "the greatest end in Alabama history and that includes Don Hutson," declared Bear Bryant, who went on to call Newsome "the best athlete we've had at Alabama since Joe Namath." From 1974-77, split end/tight end Newsome started in 48 straight games and caught 102 passes for 2,070 yards. The Tide won three SEC titles during that time.

After the 1977 season, the All-American was drafted by the Cleveland Browns and became the leading receiver in franchise history. He eventually was named Alabama's Player of the Decade for the '70s and was inducted into the Alabama sports, the college football, and the pro football, halls of fame. He became the NFL's first African-American general manager.

But Newsome didn't start out as a kid very interested in football. He didn't go out for football until he was in the eighth grade. His first day, "he showed up late, didn't know what he was doing and had no idea what position he wanted to play." The first position he played was wide receiver. "That's where I stayed." In high school, the greater demands and expectations surrounding football left him determined to "play out the schedule and quit after the season" to dedicate himself to baseball and basketball.

Fortunately for Alabama gridiron history, his plans changed in the first game of his varsity career when he scored a touchdown on the first pass he caught. He was hooked. "The story begins" was how "The Wizard of Oz" described his change of plans.

To be unable to adapt to changing circumstances to is stultify and die. It's true of animal life, of business and industry, of the military, of sports teams, of you and your relationships, your job, and your finances.

Since you manage to function quite well as a cog in the complex machinery that is American society today, you change your plans regularly enough to make it routine for you. But consider how remarkable it is that the God of the universe may change his mind about something. What could bring that about?

Prayer. Someone -- an old nomad named Abraham or a 21st-century Alabama fan like you -- talks to God, who listens and considers what is asked of him.

You may feel uncomfortable praying. Maybe you're reluctant and embarrassed; perhaps you feel you're not very good at it. But nobody majors in prayer at school, and as for being reluctant, what have you got to lose? Your answer may even be a change of plans on God's part. Such is the power of prayer.

All I knew is that when they threw it, I would catch it.
-- Ozzie Newsome on his first experience with football

Prayer is so powerful it may even change God's mind.

DAY 77

GOOD LUCK

Read 1 Samuel 28:3-20.

"Saul then said to his attendants, 'Find me a woman who is a medium, so I may go and inquire of her'" (v. 7).

Antoine Pettway wasn't superstitious, but it sure was nice to have those ugly red shoes back.

The walk-on point guard, whom Coach Mark Gottfried called "the heart and soul" of the most successful men's basketball team in school history, had worn a ghastly pair of ruby red basketball sneakers during the Tide's run to the SEC championship in the 2001-02 season. He retired them only because they wore out.

After the Tide upset top-seed Stanford in the second round of the 2004 NCAA Tournament (See Devotion No. 49.), Pettway asked Director of Basketball Operations Darron Boatright if he could find another pair of those ugly red shoes, which had been discontinued. Boatright just happened to have a pair on hand. The coaches had ordered two pairs of red shoes for Pettway when they learned he was borrowing that style of shoe from teammate Rod Grizzard, whose foot was a size bigger.

Boatright said the coaches kept the last pair, waiting for Pettway to show interest in them. So the shoes sat silently in the equipment room in Tuscaloosa until the senior inquired about them after pulling off repeated heroics in the win over Stanford and prior to the Sweet Sixteen match-up with Syracuse. Pettway got his red shoes back. Teammate Earnest Shelton remarked, "Pett

CRIMSON TIDE

might come out and have a monster game now."

Considering Pettway's toughness and competitive nature, the ugly shoes didn't have much to do with what happened against Syracuse. He had ten points, nine assists, and not a single turnover as the Tide beat the defending national champions 80-71 and advanced to the Elite Eight for the first time in school history.

Black cats are right pretty. A medium is a steak. A key chain with a rabbit's foot wasn't too lucky for the rabbit. And what in the world is a blarney stone? About as superstitious as you get is to say "God bless you" when somebody sneezes.

You look indulgently upon good-luck charms, tarot cards, astrology, palm readers, and the like; they're really just amusing and harmless. So what's the problem? Nothing as long as you conduct yourself with the belief that superstitious objects and rituals – from broken mirrors to your daily horoscope – can't bring about good or bad luck. You aren't willing to let such notions and nonsense rule your life.

Superstition can be sneakily dangerous, though, because without your even realizing what's happening, it can lure you into trusting it. You thus allow it some degree of influence over your life. In that case, it subverts God's rightful place.

Whether or not it's superstition, something does rule your life. It should be God – and God alone.

Few people on this planet are more superstitious than professional athletes.

-- *Jake Monroe,* ChaCha Sports

**Superstitions may not rule your life, but
something does; it should be God and God alone.**

DAY 78

STORM WARNING

Read Luke 12:4-10.

"Whoever acknowledges me before men, the Son of Man will also acknowledge him before the angels of God. But he who disowns me before men will be disowned before the angels of God" (vv. 8-9).

Don't go! Don't go in there!" With those frantic words, senior end Baxter Booth issued a warning to his teammates.

After J.B. Whitworth was fired as Alabama's head football coach in 1957, some Tide players prayed that Bear Bryant would not be hired. "The one we didn't want was Bryant," junior tackle Chuck Allen said. "All we knew about him was, man, he's tough."

The players had no idea. It started right away with the initial workout in the wrestling room. Players went into the room by position with centers and ends first. Allen and the other players stood around in their sweats waiting; no one had any idea what was happening.

Finally, the door opened and Booth came out. Allen said, "He is bleeding from his nose and his ear, and he's got vomit all down the front of his sweatshirt." That was shocking enough, but then Booth shouted, "Don't go! Don't go in there! They'll kill you! Don't go in that room!"

They had been warned, but the uneasy players went inside anyway. Allen said they all left the room "in the same sorry state: covered in their own blood and vomit. It was brutal."

CRIMSON TIDE

It stayed brutal for months. Jack Rutledge, who later played on the 1961 national champions and coached under Bryant, said he quit every day in his mind that first year. After a workout, he said, "You would have to lean against the wall and slide down to sit down, and you'd probably stay there thirty or forty minutes without moving – totally exhausted."

No one can say they hadn't been warned.

We spend a great deal of money for equipment and personnel to warn us of impending disasters. A tornado warning makes us wary. Our nation has a whole system devoted to different levels of warning about the possibility of a terrorist attack. At railroad crossings, signals with their flashing lights and clanging bells warn us of an approaching train.

We are ever on the alert for the warning signs of health problems such as cancer, heart attack, and stroke. Counselors speak of the warning signs of a distressed marriage, an unhealthy relationship, or an addiction.

We heed or ignore these various warnings in direct relation to the sense of urgency they carry for us. No warning, however, should be as urgent for all of us as the one Jesus Christ issued. In his matter-of-fact way, Jesus warned us: Claim him during our life and be claimed as God's own in Heaven; reject him and be banned from Heaven.

We've been warned.

I just wanted to live through [the] day.
-- Chuck Allen on 1958's workouts

**Jesus warned us that if we reject him here
on Earth, he will reject us in Heaven.**

DAY 79

PRESSURE COOKER

Read 1 Kings 18:16-40.

"Answer me, O Lord, answer me, so these people will know that you, O Lord, are God" (v. 37).

National title. Conference championship. Heck, even the state title. They were all on the line. Talk about pressure! The Tide responded with a drive for the ages.

On Nov. 27, 2009, Auburn and Alabama got together and staged one of the greatest Iron Bowls ever. Entering the fourth quarter, Auburn led 21-20. With 10:37 left, Alabama punted from its own end zone, and Auburn had good field position. The pressure was on the Tide defense, and they got a stop, forcing an Auburn punt that gave Alabama the ball at its own 21 with 8:27 left.

The pressure of the whole season now sat squarely upon the shoulders of the Crimson Tide offense. Auburn had effectively shut down Mark Ingram and the Alabama rushing attack; he had only 30 yards for the night. But as Ingram said, "You have to pick your medicine. If you want to stop one thing, we have to execute other aspects."

Those "other aspects" turned out to be quarterback Greg McElroy and the passing game. After freshman Trent Richardson bolted for seven, McElroy moved the chains with a third-down completion to Julio Jones. A screen to Ingram and a catch by Jones netted another first down. McElroy to Jones for eleven, McElroy to Jones for seven, and a screen pass to Richardson for 17. The

CRIMSON TIDE

Tide was sitting at the Auburn 11.

With third and four, Coach Nick Saban took a gamble. He called time out to set up a pass play. Moreover, he put senior running back Roy Upchurch into the game. He had played little because of injuries, but this was his moment. McElroy hit him in the end zone with a strike, the first touchdown catch of his career.

The Tide won 26-21. What pressure?

You live every day with pressure. As Elijah did so long ago, you lay it on the line with everybody watching. Your family, coworkers, or employees – they depend on you. You know the pressure of a deadline, of a job evaluation, of taking the risk of asking someone to go out with you, of driving in rush-hour traffic when you have to be somewhere at a certain time.

Help in dealing with daily pressure is readily available, and the only price you pay for it is your willingness to believe. God will give you the grace to persevere if you ask prayerfully.

/And while you may need some convincing, the pressures of daily living are really small potatoes since they all will pass. The real pressure comes when you stare into the face of eternity because what you do with it is irrevocable and forever. You can handle that pressure easily enough by deciding for Jesus. Eternity is then taken care of; the pressure's off – forever.

Put me in! Put me in! I just had the feeling that I'd be wide open in the end zone.

-- *Roy Upchurch*

**The greatest pressure you face in life
concerns where you will spend eternity,
which can be dealt with by deciding for Jesus.**

DAY 80

ON THE MONEY

Read Luke 16:1-15.

"You cannot serve both God and money" (v. 13b).

You can make more money playing football. With that declaration from Bear Bryant, Ken Stabler gave up playing baseball at Alabama to concentrate on football.

Among the Crimson Nation faithful, Stabler may well be the most famous former player of them all. From 1998-2007, he served as the color commentator for Alabama football radio broadcasts. "Traveling with the Snake is like being on the road with a rock star," his partner, Eli Gold, once said.

Stabler came to Tuscaloosa in 1964. He became a full-time starter in 1966 and led Alabama to a perfect season and a 34-7 blowout of Nebraska in the Sugar Bowl. He was the game's MVP.

Perhaps Stabler's most glorious moment at Alabama came in the 1967 Iron Bowl. "I played fifteen years of pro football and that's the worst weather I've ever played in," he said. "The field was six inches deep in mud and water. And it was real, real windy." Auburn led 3-0 until Stabler pulled off the famous "Run in the Mud"; he ran the option, saw a hole, and sloshed through it. "I just went straight for that chain-link fence!" Stabler said.

Stabler went on to fame and riches in the NFL with a career that saw him honored twice as the AFC player of the year.

All that money and all that fame was ahead of him, though, when Bryant showed up at his house in Foley. If the Bear came in person and "charmed your mom and dad, it was pretty much a done deal." Bryant didn't deliver a recruiting pitch; he just talked about hunting and fishing. "That was it!" Stabler recalled.

He wanted to play baseball and football at Alabama, but the broke country boy had dreams of great riches. When Bryant said he'd make more money playing football, his inchoate baseball career came to end. A coach arranged for him to get a job mowing lawns to put some change in his pocket.

Having a little too much money at the end of the month may be as bothersome -- if not as worrisome -- as having a little too much month at the end of the money. The investment possibilities are bewildering: stocks, bonds, mutual funds, that group pooling their money to open up a neighborhood coffee shop -- that's a good idea.

You take your money seriously, as well you should. Jesus, too, took money seriously, warning us frequently of its dangers. Money itself is not evil; its peril lies in the ease with which it can usurp God's rightful place as the master of our lives.

Certainly in our age and society, we often measure people by how much money they have. But like our other talents, gifts, and resources, money should primarily be used for God's purposes. God's love must touch not only our hearts but our wallets also.

How much of your wealth are you investing with God?

Money can buy you everything but happiness. It can pay your fare to everywhere but heaven.

-- Pete Maravich

**Your attitude about money says much
about your attitude toward God.**

DAY 81

THE SUB

Read Galatians 3:10-14.

"Christ redeemed us from the curse of the law by becoming a curse for us" (v. 13).

In one of the most important games in Alabama basketball history, the subs refused to play.

In 1956, Tide coach Johnny Dee's "Rocket 8" lineup was on a collision course with Kentucky. Under Adolph Rupp, the Wildcats ruled college basketball. But when they met on Feb. 25, 1956, Alabama was 10-0 in the SEC and had won twelve in a row; Kentucky was 10-1 in the conference.

The two teams scratched and clawed the first half with the Tide leading at the break 43-40. Three minutes into the second half, Kentucky led 51-50. And then something happened that fans with long memories will never forget.

All-American forward George Linn hit a jumper, knocked down two free throws, and then put a rebound back up for two. Inspired, his teammates caught fire too, and quickly the score ran to 64-50. And the points kept coming.

With nine minutes left, Bama led 78-52; the Rocket 8 had outscored Kentucky 28-1 in about seven minutes.

The whole place was in an uproar as the Tide kept making baskets. Into the 80s. And the 90s. The game well in hand, Dee decided to pull his starters, to let everybody take part in the fun. As it turned out, though, the subs launched a full-fledged revolt.

CRIMSON TIDE

Despite some earnest conversations from their animated coach, they refused to go in. They wanted to play, sure, but they wanted something else even more. As one of the subs told Dee, "Aw, coach, let 'em stay out there, and get a hundred. This one is theirs."

Seventeen seconds remained when Linn stole a pass and drove for a layup to make the final score 101-77. For the first time in history, a team had scored one hundred points on Kentucky.

Wouldn't it be cool if you had a substitute to take care of life's hard stuff? Telling of a death in the family? Call in your sub. Breaking up with your boyfriend? Job interview? Chemistry test? Crucial presentation at work? Let the sub handle it.

We do have such a substitute, but not for the matters of life. Instead, Jesus is our substitute for matters of life and death. Since Jesus has already made it, we don't have to make the sacrifice God demands for forgiveness and salvation.

One of the ironies of our age is that many people desperately grope for a substitute for Jesus. Mysticism, human philosophies such as Scientology, false religions such as Hinduism and Islam, cults, New Age approaches that preach self-fulfillment and inner peace without any corresponding responsibility or accountability – they and others like them are all pitiful, inadequate, and hollow substitutes for Jesus.

Accept no substitutes. It's Jesus or nothing.

I never substitute just to substitute. The only way a guy gets off the floor is if he dies.
— Former Basketball Coach Abe Lemons

There is no substitute for Jesus,
the consummate substitute.

PROUD OF IT

Read 1 John 2:15-17.

"Everything in the world -- the desire of the flesh, the desire of the eyes, the pride in riches -- comes not from the Father but from the world" (v. 16 NRSV).

On an October afternoon after a game, an opposing player calmly and matter-of-factly spoke what were probably the most painful words Bear Bryant ever heard during his storied career.

In 1969, after Tennessee waxed the Tide 41-14, Steve Kiner, an All-American linebacker, said to Bryant, "Gee, Coach, they don't seem to have the same pride in wearing that red jersey anymore." If an opponent could see it, so could Bryant, and he admitted that something had happened to the program. "We kind of lost something the last two years," he said.

In his usual thorough way, after the 1970 season and two straight five-loss seasons, Bryant set out to make things right again in Tuscaloosa, instituting a number of changes that amounted to a virtual overhaul of the way Alabama played football. The changes brought immediate results in 1971 in the form of wins; 11-point favorite USC, Southern Mississippi, and then Florida all fell. By then, Alabama was ranked in the top ten.

The true measure of whether the pride was back and of how far the Tide had come came in Birmingham on Oct. 9, 1971, when Alabama took on an undefeated Ole Miss team. The Tide pushed the Rebs around from the start, but led only 13-6 at halftime despite 250 yards of offense. That all changed very quickly. The first three times Alabama touched the ball in the last half, they went for touchdowns. The Tide mugged the Rebs 40-6, bulldozing for an incredible 531 yards rushing.

How far had the Tide come? The season before, Ole Miss had won 48-23; Alabama had rushed for a grand total of 27 yards.

The pride -- not to mention the wins -- was back.

What are you most proud of? The size of your bank account? The trophies from your tennis league? The title under your name at the office? Your family?

Pride is one of life's great paradoxes. You certainly want a surgeon who takes pride in her work or an Alabama coach who is proud of his team's accomplishments. But pride in the things and the people of this world is inevitably disappointing because it leads to dependence upon things that will pass away and idolization of people who will fail you. Self-pride is even more dangerous because it inevitably leads to self-glorification.

Pride in the world's baubles and its people lures you to the earthly and the temporary, and away from God and the eternal. Pride in yourself yields the same results in that you exalt yourself and not God. God alone is glorious enough to be worshipped. Jesus Christ alone is Lord.

Southerners are proud of their football heritage, their schools, and their teams. And they share a deep pride that goes with being from the South.
-- Announcer George Mooney

Pride can be dangerous because it tempts you to lower your sight from God and the eternal to the world and the temporary.

DAY 83

A LONG SHOT

Read Matthew 9:9-13.

"[Jesus] saw a man named Matthew sitting at the tax collector's booth. 'Follow me,' he told him, and Matthew got up and followed him" (v. 9).

No batting cage, stadium, or equipment shed. The whole program only three years old. And this team is going to make it to the Women's College World Series. You've kidding, right?

That was the situation in 2000 as head coach Patrick Murphy and his Crimson Tide softball team prepared for its fourth season of play. The squad had never had a batting cage, getting its first one as the season began. They had played at two city recreation parks before finally getting a home stadium for the fourth season. And the equipment shed was Murphy's car. He lugged bats and balls to January practices while the stadium was under construction, his team practicing despite the distraction of the "war zone" sound of hammers and saws.

Given that situation, an impartial critic would have had to admit that Alabama was at best a long shot to play its way into the softball world series. Not even all the players were convinced they could make it. When first-team All-SEC pitcher Shelley Laird of the 37-6 record and the 1.37 ERA was asked when she thought the Tide was good enough to make the world series, she replied, "This weekend." That was the weekend the squad actually made it to the women's world series by stunning powerhouse Arizona

State twice in Tempe in a 4-0 sweep of the regional tournament.

"The reporters in Arizona couldn't believe it," Murphy said. Their dismay at Alabama's success was understandable since nobody beat the-then Pac 10 in softball. UCLA and Arizona alone had won 11 of the past 12 national championships. But there was the Tide, the No. 5 seed among the eight teams, only the second SEC team ever to reach the series. The long shot had made it.

Matthew the tax collector was another long shot, an unlikely person to be a confidant of the Son of God. While we may not get all warm and fuzzy about the IRS, our government's revenue agents are nothing like Matthew and his ilk. He bought a franchise, paying the Roman Empire for the privilege of extorting, bullying, and stealing everything he could from his own people. Tax collectors of the time were "despicable, vile, unprincipled scoundrels."

And yet, Jesus said only two words to this lowlife: "Follow me." Jesus knew that this long shot would make an excellent disciple.

It's the same with us. While we may not be quite as vile as Matthew was, none of us can stand before God with our hands clean and our hearts pure. We are all impossibly long shots to enter God's Heaven. That is, until we do what Matthew did: get up and follow Jesus.

[Playing in the World Series in 2000] shows how far this program has come in such a short amount of time.

-- Tide Center Fielder Kelly Kretschman

Only through Jesus does our status change
from being long shots to enter God's Kingdom
to being heavy favorites.

DAY 84

WHO, ME?

Read Judges 6:11-23.

"'But Lord,' Gideon asked, 'how can I save Israel? My clan is the weakest in Manasseh, and I am the least in my family'" (v. 15).

Steve Sloan was just minding his own business, reading the newspaper, when he got the surprise of his life. There it was in black and white: He was the starting quarterback for Alabama in the Sugar Bowl.

Sloan was an All-American quarterback who led the Tide to two SEC and national championships. In his sophomore season of 1963, though, he was a starting defensive back who played little at quarterback. That was quite understandable since the starter was a guy named Joe Namath and the backup was a capable guy named Jack Hurlbut.

Thus, Sloan didn't expect to see any time under center when the team traveled to New Orleans after a 9-2 season to play Ole Miss in the Sugar Bowl. Not even when Bryant suspended Namath late in the season did Sloan have hopes of playing much. Everyone -- including Sloan -- expected Hurlbut to start.

Boy, was he in for a surprise. And he didn't even hear about it from Bear Bryant. "I thought Jack was going to be the quarterback in the game and I was going to be in the secondary, where I had been," Sloan said. He had actually had a good season. He enjoyed playing cornerback and watching Namath play. He admitted he was nervous when he did get some playing time at quarterback while he was never anxious about playing defensive back.

But there he was -- to his surprise -- making his first collegiate start in a bowl game. The move must have surprised the coaching staff too, which overlooked naming a replacement for Sloan on defense. He played the whole first half at cornerback before the coaches realized what was happening and put someone in.

Alabama won 12-7 on four Tim Davis field goals.

You probably know exactly how Steve Sloan felt, though sometimes the moment of surprise -- that "Who, me?" feeling -- isn't as particularly welcome for you as it was for him. How about that time the teacher called on you when you hadn't done a lick of homework? Or the night the hypnotist pulled you out of a room full of folks to be his guinea pig? You've had the wide-eyed look and the turmoil in your midsection when you were suddenly singled out and found yourself in a situation you neither sought nor were prepared for.

You may feel the same way Gideon did about being called to serve God in some way, quailing at the very notion of being audacious enough to teach Sunday school, lead a small group study, or coordinate a high school prayer club. After all, who's worthy enough to do anything like that?

The truth is that nobody is – but that doesn't seem to matter to God. And it's his opinion, not yours, that counts.

I just know it caught me by surprise.
* -- Steve Sloan on his being named starter for the 1964 Sugar Bowl.*

You're right in that no one is worthy to serve God,
but the problem is that doesn't matter to God.

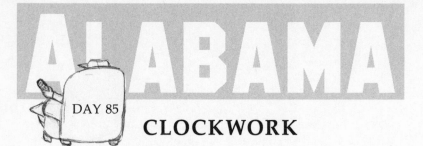
CLOCKWORK

Read Matthew 25:1-13.

"Keep watch, because you do not know the day or the hour" (v. 13).

All the Tide was trying to do was run out the clock. All they did was pull off one of the longest touchdown drives ever.

On Saturday, Nov. 16, 2002, in Baton Rouge, the 10th-ranked Crimson Tide led 14th-ranked LSU 6-0 with only 1:53 left in the half. Against the country's top-ranked defense, the Tide had managed only 129 total yards. So when the offense trotted onto the field with the ball sitting at the Alabama four with only one timeout left, their instructions were clear: Make a first down and run out the clock; get out of the cold into a warm dressing room with that six-point lead.

A funny thing happened, though. Coach Dennis Franchione and offensive coordinator Les Koenning called for a little delay handoff to tailback Santonio Beard. He got twelve yards; that was good; the clock could run. So they called that play again. 19 yards this time. Then, on third down, Shaud Williams got the delay handoff and 18 yards. With LSU concentrating on the option, the draw play was eating up chunks of yardage.

The ball was on LSU's 47 with 42 seconds left, and the goal changed. Suddenly, the team was thinking three points. On second down, the Tide called that same draw play and Williams exploded for 32 yards to the Tiger 14. Quarterback Tyler Watts spiked the ball to stop the clock with 22 seconds left.

The goal had changed again. A touchdown suddenly seemed quite possible. This time the Tide really crossed LSU up by running the option the Tigers had been trying to defend. Watts got nine yards and a penalty on a late hit. From the two, he kept it again and scored. When Triandos Luke added the conversion on an end around, Alabama led 14-0 at halftime.

Trying to run out the clock, the Tide had driven 96 yards in 101 seconds. LSU never recovered; Alabama won 31-0.

We may pride ourselves on our time management, but the truth is that we don't manage time; it manages us. Hurried and harried, we live by schedules that seem to have too much what and too little when. By setting the bedside alarm at night, we even let the clock determine how much down time we get. A life of leisure actually means one in which time is of no importance.

Every second of our life – all the time we have – is a gift from God, who dreamed up time in the first place. We would do well, therefore, to consider what God considers to be good time management. After all, Jesus himself warned us against mismanaging the time we have.

From God's point of view, using our time wisely means being prepared at every moment for Jesus' return, which will occur -- well, only time will tell when.

Les Koenning and I just talked about getting a first down.
  – Coach Dennis Franchione on the strategy that preceded the drive

We mismanage our time
when we fail to prepare for Jesus' return
even though we don't know when that will be.

DAY 86

FOR ALL YOU KNOW

Read John 8:12-32.

"You will know the truth, and the truth will set you free"
(v. 32).

Crimson Tide pinch runner Jeff Texada couldn't believe what his third-base coach, Dax Norris, was doing, But Norris knew something Texada didn't, and the result was a key Alabama win.

On Sunday, May 11, 2008, Alabama and Florida squared off in the final game of a weekend series. The race for berths in the eight-team SEC tournament was so tight that for Alabama a loss meant a fall as far as eighth place in the league and a win meant a rise to fourth place.

Florida seemed to have the game in hand with a 7-2 lead headed into the bottom of the eighth inning. But with two outs, outfielder Kent Matthes, who would be Alabama's first-ever SEC Player of the Year, blasted a three-run homer. Del Howell and Jake Smith singled, and Tyler Odle tripled them home. The game was tied.

After Florida failed to score in the top of the ninth, catcher Alex Avila was hit by a pitch and replaced by Texada. Brandon May stroked his fourth single of the game, leaving runners at first and second with one out. First-baseman Matt Bentley then lofted a sacrifice fly. Texada tagged up at second and raced toward third, prepared to come to a stop. That's when he could not believe what he saw: Norris was waving him home. "I was questioning, 'Why?'" he said. But he did what his coach ordered and slid in headfirst

at home with the game-winning run.

So what led Morris to make what was an unlikely call? First, he knew that the Florida right fielder had missed the cutoff man, giving Texada a chance to score. He also knew something else: If Alabama didn't score right then and there, the game would end in a tie because of the SEC's curfew rule for Sunday afternoon games. Morris knew it -- and Alabama had what coach Jim Wells called the most important win of the season.

Like Jeff Texada against Florida, there's much you just flat don't know. Maybe it's the formula for the area of a cylinder or the capital of Myanmar. You may not know how paper is made from trees. Or how toothpaste gets into the tube. And can you honestly say you know how the opposite sex thinks?

Despite your ignorance about certain subjects, you manage quite well because what you don't know generally doesn't hurt you too much. In certain aspects of your life, though, ignorance is anything but harmless. Imagine, for instance, the consequence of not knowing how to do your job. Or of getting behind the wheel without knowing how to drive a car.

In your faith life, what you don't know can have awful, eternal consequences. To willfully choose not to know Jesus is to be condemned to an eternity apart from God. When it comes to Jesus, knowing the truth sets you free; on the other hand, ignoring the truth about Jesus enslaves you.

With that situation -- curfew, two outs -- make him throw you out.
  – Coach Dax Norris on his decision to send Jeff Texada home

**What you don't know may not hurt you
except when it comes to Jesus.**

DAY 87

STOP, THIEF!

Read Exodus 22:1-15

"A thief must certainly make restitution" (v. 2b).

Lee Roy Jordan's mom was such a good cook that she inspired a little larceny "in the heart of an otherwise honest young man" who would go on to become Alabama's athletic director.

Bear Bryant called Jordan "the finest player I ever coached" and "one of the finest football players the world has ever seen." From 1960-62, Jordan played linebacker for the Tide. He was All-America and Alabama's defensive player of the decade.

Jordan simply loved football. Growing up on a family farm in South Alabama had a lot to do with that. "I grew up picking cotton on my daddy's farm," he said. "To me, football is like a day off." The Jordan family farm raised just about everything the family ate. "We basically bought flour, salt and pepper," Jordan said.

Mal Moore, who became Alabama's Director of Athletics in November 1999, was a teammate of Jordan's. "I went home with Lee Roy once and spent a weekend with his family," Moore recalled. What he remembered most of all about the trip was that Jordan's mother "made the best pecan pies ever."

After a trip home, Jordan came back in and "left a big slice of that pecan pie on his cabinet and went out on a date." Moore came in before Jordan did and spotted that pie. He couldn't resist. More than that, he turned it into a real treat. "I actually went over to a little cafeteria nearby and bought a pint of milk" and ate that pie and drank that milk.

Jordan showed up later with his own quart of milk and plans to wolf down some pie, which, of course, wasn't there. When he asked Moore if he had seen anyone in his room, Moore technically didn't lie when he said he hadn't. Moore finally fessed up to the theft "20 or 30 years later, when I didn't think he would care anymore, . . . and he still got real upset over it."

Buckle up your seat belt. Wear a bicycle or motorcycle helmet. Use your pooper scooper to clean up after your dog. Don't walk on the grass. Picky ordinances, picky laws – in all their great abundance, they're an inescapable part of our modern lives.

When Moses came stumbling down Mt. Sinai after spending time as God's secretary, he brought with him a whole mess of laws and regulations, many of which undoubtedly seem picky to us today. What some of them provide, though, are practical examples of what for God is the basic principle underlying the theft of personal property: what is wrong must be made right.

While it's likely that most of us today probably won't have to worry too much about oxen, sheep, and donkeys, making what is wrong right remains a way of life for Christians. To get right with other people requires anything from restitution to apologies. To get right with God requires Jesus Christ.

When we played softball, I'd steal second base, feel guilty, and go back.
-- Woody Allen

To make right the wrong of stealing requires restitution; to make right our relationship with God requires Jesus Christ.

DAY 88

GOOD SPORTS

Read Titus 2:1-8.

"Show integrity, seriousness and soundness of speech that cannot be condemned, so that those who oppose you may be ashamed because they have nothing bad to say about us" (vv. 7b, 8).

Once upon a time, the campus newspaper chided Alabama students for their poor sportsmanship at basketball games: They razzed the opposing team! Imagine students doing such a thing.

This was the same publication that classically described Alabama's play in a blowout loss to Kentucky in 1926: "Every man played a pretty floor game, in that they were all flat on the floor most of the time."

The early days of Alabama basketball featured a game quite different from the one we know today. Opponents included the likes of the Birmingham Athletic Club, the Montgomery YMCA, and the Naval Training Station. Players used a two-handed set shot and generally weren't very tall.

The age had different notions of what made for good sportsmanship too, as demonstrated by a 1927 editorial in the *Crimson-White*. The editor declared that at the recent basketball games, "a large number of students have conducted themselves in a manner which reflects discredit, not only upon themselves, but upon the fair name of the University of Alabama."

And what awful things did these miscreants do? "Not content

with 'booing' and 'hissing' the referee, . . . these students have done everything in their power to distract the attention of the visiting players while they are attempting to shoot fouls."

The writer went on to huff that the opponents "are the guests of the University and the student body, and as such merit every possible courtesy at the hands of the student body. The 'razzing' of visiting players is a most despicable practice."

And just plain old poor sportsmanship too.

One of life's paradoxes is that many who would never consider cheating on the tennis court or the racquetball court think nothing of doing so in other areas of their life. In other words, the good sportsmanship they practice on the golf course or even on the Monopoly board doesn't carry over. They play with the truth, cut corners, abuse others verbally, run roughshod over the weaker, and generally cheat whenever they can to gain an advantage on the job or in their personal relationships.

But good sportsmanship is a way of living, not just of playing. Shouldn't you accept defeat without complaint (You don't have to like it.); win gracefully without gloating; treat your competition with fairness, courtesy, generosity, and respect? That's the way one team treats another in the name of sportsmanship. That's the way one person treats another in the name of Jesus.

One person practicing sportsmanship is better than a hundred teaching it.

-- Knute Rockne

Sportsmanship -- treating others with courtesy, fairness, and respect -- is a way of living, not just a way of playing.

PAYBACK

Read Matthew 5: 38-42.

"I tell you, Do not resist an evil person. If someone strikes you on the right cheek, turn to him the other also" (v. 39).

Alabama players and fans waited a full year, but the wait was well worth it as they paid Florida back with a quite thorough and totally humiliating beatdown.

One of the more painful memories the Tide faithful lugged around for a year was the fact that their beloved and undefeated team had actually led Florida 20-17 going into the fourth quarter of the 2008 SEC championship game. But in the final period Alabama netted one yard of total offense while the Gators scored twice and won 31-20. The Crimson Tide Nation could then only watch Florida win the national championship that they had had virtually within their grasp.

"It wasn't going to happen again," declared left guard Mike Johnson as the same two teams squared off in the 2009 SEC title game. "We had a hunger." The hunger was for payback, to inflict upon the top-ranked Gators the pain and heartache they had felt the season before.

And the Tide got their revenge. Oh, did they ever.

From the opening snap, Alabama dominated, humiliated, and thoroughly whipped the Gators, blasting them 32-13. The game's MVP was a quarterback, but not the Florida one. Instead, Greg McElroy claimed the prize after throwing for 239 yards.

CRIMSON TIDE

"Everybody was talking about [Tim] Tebow going off, but today it was McElroy," said receiver Marquis Maze.

Florida was still in the game at halftime, trailing only 19-13, but there was to be no late comeback this year. The Gators would not score in the last half. The Tide had its sweet payback and eventually its even sweeter national championship.

The very nature of an intense rivalry such as the Iron Bowl and those Alabama-Florida matchups in the SEC championship games is that the loser will seek payback for the defeat of the season before. But what about in life when somebody's done you wrong; is it time to get even?

The problem with revenge in real-life is that it isn't as clear-cut as a scoreboard. Life is so messy that any attempt at revenge is often inadequate or, worse, backfires and injures you.

As a result, you remain gripped by resentment and anger, which hurts you and no one else. You poison your own happiness while that other person goes blithely about her business. The only way someone who has hurt you can keep hurting you is if you're a willing participant.

But it doesn't have to be that way. Jesus ushered in a new way of living when he taught that we are not to seek revenge for personal wrongs and injuries. Let it go and go on with your life. What a relief!

Everything we did all year long was to beat [Florida].

-- Mark Ingram

Resentment and anger over a wrong injures you,
not the other person, so forget it
-- just as Jesus taught.

DAY 90

THE GREATEST

Read Mark 9:33-37.

"If anyone wants to be first, he must be the very last, and the servant of all" (v. 35).

More than thirty years after the fact, for the serious student of Alabama football history, it may well still be the greatest play in the school's storied gridiron history.

Barry Krauss has never forgotten it; it remains "the defining hour of his youth." On Jan. 1, 1979, Krauss made what has been called "the biggest tackle of the Bear Bryant era at Alabama."

A two-time All-America, Krauss was a senior linebacker when the Tide met Penn State in the Sugar Bowl New Year's night. In a day long before the BCS, this was a national championship showdown: No. 1 vs. No. 2.

Alabama led 14-7 late in the fourth quarter, but the Nittany Lions recovered a Tide fumble at the 19 and quickly moved to a first down at the eight. A run and a pass put the ball inside the one on third down. Krauss, the defensive captain, called the play that sent every defender crashing into the middle to stop a run. It worked; linebacker Rich Wingo stopped the State fullback inches short of the goal line.

The Lions called time out. No one ever doubted they would go for the touchdown.

On the Bama sideline, defensive coordinator Ken Donahue called for the same defense that had stopped Penn State on third down. He was convinced the Nittany Lions would try to power the ball in again. They did.

At the snap, All-American defensive tackle Marty Lyons single-handedly surged and collapsed the Penn State line. Wingo hit the lead blocker. When the runner tried to leap over the pile, Krauss met him "face mask to face mask." "I actually broke my helmet," Krauss recalled. "When I hit him, it took everything out of me."

The Tide had held with its greatest play ever.

We all want to be the greatest. The goal for the Crimson Tide and their fans every season is the national championship. The competition at work is to be the most productive sales person on the staff or the Teacher of the Year. In other words, we define being the greatest in terms of the struggle for personal success. It's nothing new; the disciples saw greatness in the same way.

As Jesus illustrated, though, greatness in the Kingdom of God has nothing to do with the world's understanding of success. Rather, the greatest are those who channel their ambition toward the furtherance of Christ's kingdom through love and service, rather than their own advancement, which is a complete reversal of status and values as the world sees them.

After all, who could be greater than the person who has Jesus for a brother and God for a father? And that's every one of us.

To think I made an impact or was part of an incredible moment in the history of Alabama, it's just fantastic.

-- Barry Krauss

**To be great for God has nothing to do
with personal advancement and everything to do
with the advancement of Christ's kingdom.**

THINK ABOUT IT

Read Job 28.

"The fear of the Lord -- that is wisdom, and to shun evil is understanding" (v. 28).

While Barrett Jones had the necessary physical attributes to be a great offensive lineman, his ability to think on the field ultimately separated him from everyone else.

The mere sight of Barrett Jones -- all 6-foot-5, 302 lbs. of him -- and his "startling athleticism for a man his size" confounded Alabama's opponents from 2009-2012 across three national titles. Jones left Tuscaloosa as a three-time All-America and the "most versatile offensive lineman in Crimson Tide history." He won the Outland Trophy as the nation's best interior lineman in 2011 playing left tackle and then won the Rimington Trophy as college football's best center in 2012.

But even Jones admitted, "I may not be the biggest or fastest guy out there." So what was it that made him better then everybody else? He was smart. He started playing the violin when he was 3. He asked so many questions in school his third-grade teacher joked she needed a full-time assistant to answer them all. He graduated from Alabama in August 2012 with a 4.0 GPA.

He took that intellect onto the football field. Quarterback A.J. McCarron said Jones was great because he used his head. "The biggest reason our offensive line is so good is because of Barrett's intelligence," declared running back Eddie Lacy. Jones agreed with that assessment. "I like to think I have a good feel for angles and just figuring out ways to get the job done," he said.

He even called the game-winning play against LSU in 2012. With Bama trailing 17-14 late, offensive line coach Jeff Stroutland asked Jones what play they should run on their last series. "Screens have been there all night," Jones pointed out. With less than a minute on the clock, McCarron tossed a pass to T.J. Yeldon for the game-winning touchdown. It was a screen.

Like Barrett Jones, you're a thinking person. When you talk about using your head, you're speaking of using logic and reason as part of your psyche. A coach's bad call frustrates you and your children's inexplicable behavior flummoxes you. Why can't people just think things through?

That goes for matters of faith too. Jesus doesn't tell you to turn your brain off when you walk into a church or open the Bible. In fact, when you seek Jesus, you seek him heart, soul, body, and mind. The mind of the master should be the master of your mind so that you consider every situation in your life through the critical lens of the mind of Christ. With your head and your heart, you encounter God, who is, after all, the true source of wisdom.

To know Jesus is not to stop thinking; it is to start thinking divinely.

Barrett [Jones] is not only the smartest guy I know, but he's also probably the toughest.
-- Alabama left guard D.J. Fluker

Since God is the source of all wisdom,
it's only logical that you encounter him
with your mind and your emotions.

DAY 92

THE END

Read Revelation 22:1-17.

"I am the Alpha and the Omega, the First and the Last,
the Beginning and the End" (v. 13).

Bear Bryant knew the end of his coaching career was near.
What was also near the end was his life.

Bryant once said, "You're never too old until you think you
are." In 1982, he began to think he was too old to coach anymore,
declaring, "Coaching is a young man's game."

Especially in recruiting did Bryant's age -- he was 69 -- and his
health work against him and his program. He found "he could
no longer look a recruit in the eye and promise he would be there
throughout the player's career." Recruiting suffered; recruiting
coordinator Clem Gryska said, "Kids wanted to play for him, but
they were afraid he would retire while they were playing."

And so, on Dec. 15, 1982, two weeks after the regular season
ended, Bryant announced his retirement. "There comes a time in
every profession when you need to hang it up," he said. "And that
time has come." He coached his last game in the Liberty Bowl, a
21-15 win over Illinois.

More than age brought an end to Bryant's career, however. In
a closely guarded secret, his health was not good. Since 1979, he
had suffered a minor stroke and heart failure. He complained of
chest pains on the evening of Jan. 25, 1983 and was rushed to
Druid City Hospital. Doctors planned to keep him overnight for

observation.

The next morning he received a visit from his successor, former Alabama wide receiver Ray Perkins, and chided him for wasting time in the hospital when he should have been out recruiting. He checked on the scholarship of the son of a former player.

That afternoon, he was sitting up in bed eating lunch when he went into cardiopulmonary arrest. At 1:30 p.m., he was pronounced dead.

Bear Bryant's storied career and celebrated life are examples of one of life's basic truths: Everything in all of creation ends. Only God is eternal. Even the stars have a life cycle, though admittedly it's rather lengthy. Erosion eventually will wear a boulder to a pebble. Life itself is temporary; all living things have a beginning and an end.

Within the framework of our individual lifetimes, we meet endings. Loved ones, friends, and pets die; relationships fracture; jobs dry up; our own bodies, clothes, lawn mowers, TV sets – they all wear out. Even this world as we know it will end.

But one of the greatest ironies of God's gift of life is that not even death is immune from the great truth of creation that all things must end. That's because through Jesus' life, death, and resurrection, God himself acted to end any power death once had over life. In other words, because of Jesus, the end of life has ended. Eternity is ours for the claiming.

Retire? I'd probably croak in a week.

-- *Bear Bryant*

Everything on this Earth ends;
thanks to Jesus Christ, so does death.

ALABAMA

NOTES
(by Devotion Day Number)

1   Walter Shafer had been a star . . . for the football team.: Clyde Bolton, *The Crimson Tide* (Huntsville: The Strode Publishers, 1972), p. 29.

1   "In those days, football wasn't . . . and a bad limp.: Bolton, *The Crimson Tide*, p. 31.

1   "an irregular game": Bolton, *The Crimson Tide*, p. 30.

1   Older people who forget . . . will soon die out.: Bolton, *The Crimson Tide*, pp. 31-32.

2   "We can pretty much . . . Alabama a Dynasty?' debate,": Gene Wojciechowski, "Tide at Pinnacle of College Football," *ESPN.com*, Jan. 7, 2013. http://espn. go.com/college-football/bowls.

2   "Bama should get a crystal trophy and a half for this one.": Wojciechowski.

2   "beyond impressive; it's historic.": Wojciechowski.

2   "I don't think words . . . he said, is accomplishment.: Wojciechowski.

2   Dynasty. I say it all day. Unprecedented. Dynasty, man!: Wojciechowski.

3   It became known as "The Shot That Saved Lives,": Thomas Lake, "The Shot That Saved Lives," *Sports Illustrated*, March 16, 2009, http://sports illustrated.cnn.com/vault/article/magazine/MAG1153064/index.htm, Feb. 18, 2010.

3   "not a superstar, not even . . . Mykal is a shooter.": Lake.

3   In the huddle, Tide coach . . . and the horn blared.: Lake.

3   About eight minutes later, . . . the path of the storm.: Lake.

3   This was a walking crowd.: Lake.

4   "tossed the biggest curveball of the tournament.": Gentry Estes, "Hope Is Alive," *The Mobile Press-Register*, May 31, 2009, http://www.al.com/alabamabaseball/mobileregister/women.ssf?/base/sports, June 6, 2009.

4   a freshman who hadn't . . . base hit in 38 days.: Estes, Hope Is Alive."

4   I just felt good . . . a gut feeling.: Estes, "Hope Is Alive."

5   "will be debated . . . for years to come.": Todd Jones, "Title Wave," *Yea Alabama 2009* (Hanover, MA: Maple Street Press LLC, 2010), p. 11.

5   I can't believe I . . . into the end zone.: William C. Rhoden, "Dareus's Big Plays Surprised Even Him," *The New York Times*, Jan. 8, 2010, http://www.ny times.com/2010/01/09/sports/ncaafootball/09rhoden.html, Feb. 19, 2010.

6   "Alabama's first true national football star": Richard Scott, *Legends of Alabama Football* (Champaign, IL: Sports Publishing L.L.C., 2004), p. 31.

6   "shocked West Coast fans and reporters": Scott, p. 28.

6   "By having such unparalleled . . . and would honor it.: Eli Gold, *Crimson Nation* (Nashville: Rutledge Hill Press, 2005), p. 32.

6   The best you can do . . . unless it does the job.: Gold, p. 32.

7   Davidson received a call . . . gave his life to the Lord.": Grant Wahl, "Playing Through the Pain," *Sports Illustrated*, Jan. 29, 2007, http://sportsillustrated. cnn.com/vault/article/magazine/MAG1104375/index.htm, Feb. 28, 2010.

7   Nobody could tell whether . . . down Jermareo Davidson's face.: Wahl.

8   "the greatest Alabama quarterback . . . on Shields-Watkins Field.": Al Browning, *Third Saturday in October* (Nashville: Cumberland House Publishing, Inc., 2001), p. 140.

8   "Elmore tore it up.": Browning, p. 142.

8   "called a near-flawless game.": Browning, p. 140.

8   a "spy" was discovered . . . friendly their students were.: Browning, p. 143.

9   Right before two-a-days began, . . . classic hymn "Love Lifted Me": Frank
     Deford, "'I Do Love the Football,'" *Sports Illustrated*, Nov. 23, 1981, http://
     sportsillustrated.cnn.com/vault/article/magazine/MAG1125024/index.htm,
     Feb. 22, 2010.

9   "There wasn't but about three cars on campus then.": Deford.

9   He had overslept that morning . . . want to stop coaching.": Deford.

9   "I do love the football,": Deford.

9   The main thing about staying . . . you've got to want to.: Deford.

10   1,200 fans crammed . . . Alabama's "steamy" natatorium: Jerry Kirshenbaum,
     "High Tide Washes over Vols," *Sports Illustrated*, Feb. 13, 1978, http://sports
     illustrated.cnn.clom/vault/article/magazine/MAG1093316/index.htm, Feb.
     22, 2010.

10   Tennessee had purposefully . . . a drafty doorway.: Kirshenbaum.

10   The Tennessee swimmers showed . . . "most unbeloved college swim team.":
     Kirshenbaum.

11   billboards went up around town . . . new sheriff in town,": Gold, p. 91.

11   A group of local businessmen . . . what he intended to do.": Gold, p. 93.

12   "the star" of the Tide's 7-6 upset of Fordham: Bolton, *The Crimson Tide*,
     p. 159.

12   "I went in and got a kid . . . blast to the face." "Blind Golfer 'Reads' the Greens,"
     The Palm Beach Post, March 1, 1971, http://news.google.com/newspapers?
     nid=1964&dat=19710301, Feb. 24, 2010.

12   The explosion threw Boswell . . . left him permanently blinded.: "Charles A.
     Boswell," *Encyclopedia of Alabama*, http://www.encyclopediaofalabama.org/
     face/Article.jsp?id=h-1771, Feb. 24, 2010.

12   Boswell spent four months . . . teach him to play golf.: "Blind Golfer."

12   Gleason helped Boswell . . . middle of the fairway.: "Charles A. Boswell."

12   I told him to get . . . I could ever play golf.: "Blind Golfer."

13   Hood "didn't have the ability . . . until he made himself.": Clyde Bolton, *The
     Basketball Tide* (Huntsville: The Strode Publishers, 1977), p. 53.

13   The architect who designed . . . the edges of the court.: Bolton, *The Basketball
     Tide*, p. 53.

13   "the balcony got all mixed . . . the 1930 season opener.: Bolton, *The Basketball
     Tide*, pp. 53-54.

13   While a Stanford player . . . the only way he shot,": Bolton, *The Basketball Tide*,
     p. 53.

13   Life is an adventure. . . . going to happen next.: Jim & Julie S. Bettinger, *The Book
     of Bowden* (Nashville: TowleHouse Publishers, 2001), p. 74.

14   "that was the last straw . . . working on a plan.": Gold, p. 141.

14   "In the late sixties, we had been throwing the ball a lot,": Gold, p. 142.

14   Royal "had been perfecting . . . places like Texas and Oklahoma.": Gold, p. 142.

14   Bryant called and asked . . . some time with Royal.: Gold, p. 142.

14   the Alabama coach moved in . . . to go with the wishbone.": Gold, p. 143.

14   "The wishbone was a smash.": Gold, p. 146.

14   What's new? Oh, nothing.: Gold, p. 146.

15   "The coaches told me that . . . throw for a hundred.": Gold, p. 201.

15   "I was struggling," . . . and see things clearly.": Gold, p. 202.
15   He shared his faith with . . . benching served to motivate him.: Gold, p. 202.
15   I just want to thank God . . . for the University of Alabama.: Chris Warner, ed.,
        SEC Sports Quotes (Baton Rouge: CEW Enterprises, 2002), p. 30.
16   "Even though they were . . . we were right there,": Jones, p. 40.
16   "looking for the knockout . . . . knell for the Gamecocks.": Jones, p. 40.
16   Offensive coordinator Jim McElwain . . . could carry his team.: Jones, p. 40.
16   There were times when I thought . . . I stayed with it.: Jones, p. 38.
17   the size of the crowd . . . could lure from Anniston.": Doug Segrest,
        "Raising the Bar," *The Birmingham News*, March 5, 2003, p. 1-D.
17   In the basement of . . . promoted to head coach.: Segrest, "Raising the Bar."
17   We finished second nationally . . . I got sympathy cards.: Segrest, "Raising the
        Bar."
18   Nick Saban could never pinpoint . . . competitors for playing time.: Ian R.
        Rapoport, "Turning Points," *The Birmingham News*, Dec. 2, 2008, p. 1-C.
19   The kids chopped cotton . . . Nothing worked.: Scott, p. 151.
19   At the end of the day, . . . be with you forever.'": Scott, p. 152.
19   I hated Kate. Kate worked us to death.: Scott, p. 151.
20   "but the excruciating part . . . insults for a whole year.": Ray Kennedy, "Battle
        for Braggin' Rights," *Sports Illustrated*, Dec. 9, 1974, http://sportsillustrated.
        cnn.com/vault/article/magazine/MAG1089323/index.htm, Feb. 22, 2010.
20   Alabama's records consider it . . . first game of the 1893 season.: Bolton, *The
        Crimson Tide*, p. 24.
20   Auburn first pointlessly accused Alabama of cheating in 1894.: Bolton, *The
        Crimson Tide*, p. 29.
20   "I didn't mind all the phone . . . boaters squawking 'War Eagle.'": Kennedy.
20   I'd love to beat Notre Dame, . . . the other side of the state.: Warner, p. 13.
21   "The University team was greatly . . . bouncing to the floor.": Bolton, *The Basket-
        ball Tide*, p. 26.
21   Only a few paying . . . have a team next year." Bolton, *The Basketball Tide*, p. 28.
21   "the sport's lack of . . . and on the campus.": Bolton, *The Basketball Tide*, p. 33.
21   one of the games in 1916 . . . the glee club concert.": Bolton, *The Basketball Tide*,
        p. 33.
21   "The University of Alabama . . . basketball in the past.": Bolton, *The Basketball
        Tide*, p. 42.
21   Students at the university . . . popular in the North.: Bolton, *The Basketball Tide*,
        p. 42.
22   "the best coaching decision . . . the meaning of integrity.": "Joe Namath,"
        Wikipedia, the free encyclopedia, http://en.wikipedia.org/wiki/Joe_Namath,
        Feb. 24, 2010.
22   Namath struggled against Vanderbilt . . . ever do that again.'": Gold, p. 124.
22   That way also meant doling . . . proved something to me.": Gold, p. 125.
22   I deserved that suspension . . . make it 110 percent.: Gold, p. 126.
23   "I wasn't doing too well . . . grades I was making!": Scott, p. 82.
23   When the coach started talking, . . . straightened out real fast!": Scott, p. 82.
23   You hear a lot of talk . . . Coach Bryant back in 1958.: Scott, p. 82.
24   "fastest kid we've ever had on the team,": Steve Kirk, "Tide Coach Embraces
        Slap-Hitting Speedster," *The Birmingham News*, May 10, 2006, p. 1-C.
24   Tide assistant coaches Alyson . . . give each other a hug.": Kirk, "Tide Coach

Embraces."

24 [Coach Murphy] was the only . . . That won me over.": Kirk, "Tide Coach Embraces."

25 they were ready for just such . . . known as gut-check day.": Don Wade, *Always Alabama* (New York: Simon & Schuster, 2006), pp. 139-40.

25 for one hour, "you were . . . not getting in the end zone.": Wade, p. 140.

25 as the celebrating palyers . . . job well done, men.'": Wade, p. 140.

25 Man, that just sent goosebumps.: Wade, p. 140.

26 In high school, Todd had reservations . . . helped anyone else, either.": Tommy Hicks, *Game of My Life: Alabama* (Champaign, IL: Sports Publishing L.L.C., 2006), p. 90.

27 "How stupid is that?" . . . That's what Rader saw;: Steve Kirk, "Not Like They Drew It Up," *The Birmingham News*, Sept. 25, 2005, p. 1-C.

27 He glanced at Hall, . . . hauled it in: Kirk, "Not Like They Drew It Up."

27 "I didn't want to look out [at Hall] again,": Kirk, "Not Like They Drew It Up."

28 Alabama added a new starting quarterback -- to its baseball team.: Gentry Estes, "Tuscaloosa Native Chris Smelley to Transfer Schools and Sports," The *Mobile Press-Register*, Jan. 9, 2009, http://blog.al.com/bamabeat/2009/01/alabama_could_soon-be_adding.html, March 19, 2010.

28 Smelley never originally intended . . . makes me the most happy.": Ian R. Rapoport, "Smelley in On-Deck Circle for Tide," *The Birmingham News*, Feb. 18, 2009, p. 3-C.

28 battling for playing time . . . looked up and smiled.: Ray Glier, "Now Calling Pitches, Not Signals," *The New York Times*, March 4, 2009, http://www.nytimes.com/2009/03/05/sports/baseball/05smelley.html, March 19, 2010.

28 I loved playing for . . . I'm here now.: Rapoport, "Smelley in On-Deck Circle."

29 "the best offensive lineman I ever coached.": Scott, p. 125.

29 Hannah later called not . . . disappointment of his career.: Scott, p. 129.

29 "a step down from Alabama." . . . for the last three years.": Scott, p. 129.

30 "glory days at Alabama beyond [their] wildest reckoning.": Gold, p. 90.

30 "The Dark Years.": Bolton, *The Crimson Tide*, p. 187.

30 "a nice guy who was . . . that things were *bad*.": Gold, p. 88.

30 "I came here to make Alabama a winner again,": Gold, p. 91.

30 "I'm not worried about . . . this room are winners.": Scott, p. 19.

30 players showed up for practice . . . garbage pails for vomiting.: Scott, p. 18.

30 "no college football coach . . . better than Bryant.": Scott, p. 16.

30 "When the whistle blew . . . a return to glory": Gold, p. 96.

30 I ain't nothing but a winner.: Scott, p. 16.

31 the rumor circulated that . . . after being kidnapped.: Mark Beech, "The Tide Has Turned," *Sports Illustrated*, Oct. 10, 2005, http://sportsillustrated.cnn.com/vault/article/magazine/MAG1103865/index.htm, Feb. 18, 2010.

31 "made seemingly every throw . . . "Beatlemania-like.": Beech.

31 We just try to be as nice as we can and keep moving.: Beech.

32 "a disgrace to integrity" . . . have been "Leningrad Stadium.": Curry Kirkpatrick, "Solution to a Thorny Problem," *Sports Illustrated*, March 15, 1982, http://sportsillustrated.cnn.com/vault/article/magazine/MAG1125307/index.htm, Feb. 20, 2010.

32 his team was whistled . . . broke down and cried: Kirkpatrick.

32 What Wimp Sanderson did . . . a game during the season.:

Kirkpatrick.

32   Mike Davis and freshman guard . . . the ball airborne quick,": Kirkpatrick.

33   He can sell tickets too.": Hicks, p. 47.

33   Florida head coach Ray Graves . . . "to prove them wrong.": Hicks, p. 44.

33   Ray played defensive back, . . . have a favorite position.": Hicks, p. 46.

33   You played wherever you could play that would help the team.: Hicks, p. 46.

34   In 1976, Doug Barfield, . . . "What's the problem then?": Hicks, p. 122.

34   "the quickest 8 yards . . . over and celebrated too.": Hicks, p. 125.

34   A book published several . . . in Tide football history.: Hicks, p. 126.

35   The most highly recruited prospects to ever come to Alabama.": Doug Segrest, "Success Came Early for UA Duo," *The Birmingham News*, March 30, 1994, p. 1-01.

35   At her first game . . . 52 of her team's 54 points.: Segrest, "Success Came Early."

35   they had to get mentally . . . she was ready to go.: Segrest, "Success Came Early."

36   Woodrow Lowe figured the package . . . I was stunned,": Doug Segrest, "Tiger, Tider HOF Bound," *The Birmingham News*, May 1, 2009, p. 3-B.

36   Lowe's play was the source . . . a fine young man.": Segrest, "Tiger, Tider."

36   A teammate and he were . . . would have gone there.": Hicks, p. 106.

37   "I didn't see the whole play, . . . and I ran to it.": Doug Segrest, "Bama Sacks Michigan," *The Birmingham News*, Jan. 2, 1997, p. 01-C.

37   "I can't think of a more fitting game than this for Alabama and Michigan.": Segrest, "Bama Sacks Michigan."

38   A slight but steady rain . . . better than Alabama did.: Gold, p. 137.

38   "So, we're coming out of . . . on the very first play.": Gold, p. 137.

38   "We scored six or seven . . . the game was probably over.": Gold, p. 137.

39   The pundits picked Kentucky . . . in the tourney finals,: Bolton, *The Basketball Tide*, p. 59.

39   Alabama's leading scorer . . . 162 points for the season.: Bolton, *The Basketball Tide*, p. 60.

39   The squad dropped by . . . picture made with the team.: Bolton, *The Basketball Tide*, p. 61.

40   he "should become one of the greatest coaches in the country.": Scott, p. 7.

40   "one of the smartest players . . . could pick a better man,": Scott, p. 7.

40   "he was the first . . . past the season at hand.": Gold, p. 26.

40   He was the one who first . . . would be a football power.: Scott, p. vii.

40   on July 15, 1930, Denny met . . . means what he says.: Scott, pp. 7-8.

40   Those were the hardest and coldest words I ever heard.: Scott, p. 8.

41   His teamamtes were the ones . . . on him" after the national championship.: Andy Staples, "Ingram Won Heisman," *SI.com*, Jan. 5, 2010, http://sports illustrated.cnn.com/2010/writers/andy_staples/01/04/rolando-mcclain/index.htm, Jan. 6, 2010.

41   We have a low tolerance for guys who don't know what to do.: Staples.

42   Bolt was obsessed with those . . . all over the country.: Ray Melick, "A Serious Miler," *The Birmingham News*, May 28, 2009, 1-C.

42   Tide runner Bolt was a serious miler.: Melick.

42   He had run a 3:58 . . . couldn't run all the events.": Melick, "A Serious Miler."

42   Bolt's position on the team . . . as he could in everything.: Melick, A Serious Miler."

42 Looking back, I realize . . . the focus, the goals.: Melick, "A Serious Miler."

43 "I had been praying, . . . that's a smart move,": Wayne Atcheson, *Faith of the Crimson Tide* (Grand Island, NE: Cross Training Publishing, 2000), p. 210.

43 As he walked toward . . . to share that with you.": Atcheson, p. 211.

43 That was pretty amazing . . . to affirm my decision.: Atcheson, p. 211.

44 In 1958, long before integration, . . . break your word to someone.: "Bear Bryant Knew How to be Nice," *Redelephants.* http://www.redelephants. com/CoachBear Bryant.html, Feb. 24, 2010.

45 "swift, self-effacing and seamless.": Mark Heim, "Alabama Baseball Coach Jim Wells Retires after 15 Years, *The Mobile Press-Register*, Sept. 2, 2009, http:// blog.al.com/press-register-sports/2009/09/alabama_baseball_coach_jim_ wel.html, March 22, 2010.

45 Athletics Director Mal Moore tried. . . strongly about this decision.": Doug Segrest, "Wells Retires after 13 Seasons," *The Birmingham News*, June 22, 2007, p. 1-D.

45 On Wednesday after he . . . to name a replacement.: Doug Segrest, "Wells, Gaspard Would Make Good Team," *The Birmingham News*, June 28, 2007, p. 1-B.

45 "I haven't slept in . . . wanted to get it back.": Ian R. Rapaport. "Apologetic Wells Returns as Coach," *The Birmingham News*, June 28, 2007, p. 1-B.

45 I knew the decision wasn't right.: Rapaport, "Apologetic Wells Returns."

46 His dad worked in the Virginia . . . wasn't ready to sign yet.: Scott, p. 158.

46 the other two players had . . . on the dotted line with the Tide.: Scott, p. 159.

47 I'm just too full of Alabama.": Wade, p. 2.

47 The crowd of more than . . . were "momentarily mute.": Dick Heller, "Refs Didn't Cotton to Off-Bench Stop," *The Washington Times*, Jan. 1, 2007, http:// www.ricefootball.net/collegeinnwtstory.htm, March 4, 2010.

47 He had turned to a teammate . . . he sure is, Lew.": Wade, pp. 3-4.

47 "and I unloaded on him. . . . my last game at Alabama.: Wade, p. 4.

47 Lewis went to the Rice locker room and apologized,: Wade, p. 4.

47 "I don't know what got into me.": Heller.

47 The *Dallas Morning News* . . . a "forgivable error.": Wade, p. 4.

47 The ingrained philosophy . . . a little more than you've got.: Wade, p. 2.

48 "the Beatdown in TTown.": Doug Segrest, "Beatdown in T-Town," *The Birmingham News*, Nov. 30, 2008, p. 3-C.

48 the Tide players celebrated . . . to the locker room.: Segrest, "Beatdown."

48 "Our goal was to . . . That was our biggest goal.": Segrest, "Beatdown."

48 the seniors "should always . . . with a victory jig." Segrest, "Beatdown."

48 I didn't get to see . . . get that on YouTube.: Segrest, "Beatdown."

49 Mark Gottfried looked his team . . . going to win this game.: Steve Irvine, "One Is Done," *The Birmingham News*, March 21, 2004, p. 1-C.

49 Those players to whom . . . 7:42 left in the game.: Irvine, "One Is Done."

49 That shot "was big," . . . them confidence again.": Irvine, "One Is Done."

49 It gives you inspiration . . . means we can win it.: Irvine, "One Is Done."

50 At the 1987 NCAA Convention, . . . when it saw one.": Austin Murphy, "A Tidy Finish," *Sports Illustrated*, Dec. 14, 1992, http://sportsillustrated.cnn.com/ vault/article/magazine/MAG1004647/index.htm, Feb. 20, 2010.

50 themselves as playing . . . practice this week,": Murphy, "A Tidy Finish."

50   Like most men, . . . and genuinely believed in God.: Scott, p. 15.

51   They had to travel 2,500 miles . . . blowing through the train cars.": Bolton, *The Crimson Tide*, p. 56.

51   Scott "was a thinker, one of the brainiest coaches in the South.: Bolton, *The Crimson Tide*, p. 57.

51   After coaching Alabama in the fall, . . . for a Cleveland paper.: Bolton, *The Crimson Tide*, p. 53.

51   He knew his boys . . . these Eastern guys.: Bolton, *The Crimson Tide*, p. 57.

51   Before the largest crowd ever to watch an Alabama football game,: Bolton, *The Crimson Tide*, p. 57.

52   At Notre Dame, Dee typically brought . . . and brought them South.: Bolton, *The Basketball Tide*, pp. 90-91.

52   "with a slightly different . . . yelling to his facial distortions.": Bolton, *The Basketball Tide*, p. 96.

52   "A basketball player operates . . . with 60 percent efficiency.": Bolton, *The Basketball Tide*, p. 96.

52   *The Birmingham News* called Crews . . . "he's a sight.": Bolton, *The Basketball Tide*, p. 97.

53   As a quarterback, he had . . . had another like him.": Gold, p. 103.

53   "smartest and best football player [he] ever played with, period.": "Pat Trammell," *Wikipedia, the free encyclopedia*, http://en.wikipedia, org/wiki/Pat_Trammell, Feb. 23, 2010.

53   Trammell was the only guy . . . great, great, football player.": Gold, p. 104.

53   "top dog of that football team." . . . could back it up, too.": Gold, p. 103.

53   Trammell kept his freshman . . . "they all became halfbacks.": Gold, p. 104.

53   Asked in 1980 who . . . favorite *person* of my entire life.": "Pat Trammell."

53   "ambivalent, vacillating, impulsive, unsubmissive.": John MacArthur, *Twelve Ordinary Men* (Nashville: W Publishing Group, 2002), p. 39.

53   "the greatest preacher . . . in the birth of the church.: MacArthur, p. 39.

53   He was a tremendous leader. Whatever it took, he would do it.: Gold, p. 104.

54   Ingram was at best a four-star . . . or build a team around.": Pete Holiday, "On the Mark," *Yea Alabama 2009* (Hanover, MA: Maple Street Press, 2010), p. 72.

54   "At Alabama, our players . . . win national championships.": Holiday, p. 71.

55   in a Tide loss to Michigan . . . serve as her catcher.: Steve Irvine, "Laird Low-Key about SEC Record," *The Birmingham News*, Feb. 19, 2002, 6-C.

56   The whole business gave . . . and his football family.": Ward, p. 171.

56   They relied on "the word . . . inside information to Bryant.: Ward, p. 170.

56   "wanted his player to hit . . . if you did that.: Ward, p. 170.

56   the *Post* "took 10 years . . . billed them $10 million for it.": Ward, p. 169.

56   "devastated that anyone would question his integrity.": Ward, p. 171.

57   a "seven-year itch.": Steve Irvine, "Rocky Stopped," *The Birmingham News*, Oct. 27, 2002, p. 1-B.

57   "good-bye to seven . . . the crimson-clad corner": Irvine, "Rocky Stopped."

57   told the team all week . . . doubts in their mind.": Irvine, "Rocky Stopped."

57   I have been here . . . It's finally happened.: Irvine, "Rocky Stopped."

58   "I've never witnessed . . . a pressure-packed game,": Doug Segrest, "Bama Mac-Dominates Penn," *The Birmingham News*, 17 March 1995, p. 01-B.

58   their five senior starters: Segrest, "Bama Mac-Dominates."

58	scored six straight . . . for the dunk.: Segrest, "Bama Mac-Dominates."
58	"I'm not surprised,": Segrest, "Bama Mac-Dominates."
58	I was certainly impressed with Antoniio McDyess. He was awesome.: Segrest, "Bama Mac-Dominates."
59	"There are four things . . . win some football games.: Scott, p. 139.
59	"scratching my head wondering . . . were the right order.": Scott, p. 139.
59	He spent his freshman year . . . when he didn't letter,: Scott, p. 139.
59	he challenged Bryant by . . . end of my baseball career.": Scott, p. 140.
59	if he kept his priorities . . . then "good things happen.": Scott, p. 139.
59	I still try to keep those priorities in mind.: Scott, p. 139.
60	"to make the forward pass a dangerous weapon.": Scott, p. 51.
60	"with one of the greatest . . . football has ever known.: Scott, p. 53.
60	Tired of Thomas' strict . . . well, you watch.": Scott, p. 52.
60	Last night, I dreamed . . . [Alabama tackle] Bill Lee.: Scott, p. 52.
61	"We just knew we were going to win,": Todd Jones, "Run for the Roses," *Yea Alabama 2009*, Hanover, MA: Maple Street Press LLC, 2010, p. 43.
61	I just reached my arm up.: Jones, "Run for the Roses," p. 42.
62	"It felt like a funeral.": Steve Kirk, "Dead Just a Month Ago, Tide Revives," *The Birmingham News*, Feb. 11, 2006, p. 6-B.
62	"perennial cellar-dweller Ole Miss.": Kirk, "Dead Just a Month Ago."
62	"Chuck's been the heart . . . they played all 45 minutes.": Kirk, "Dead Just a Month Ago."
62	"a long, painful season remained.": Kirk, "Dead Just a Month Ago."
62	He said his guys . . . way to get there.": Kirk, "Dead Just a Month Ago."
62	the team gathered around . . . of the tournament brackets.: Steve Kirk, "Tide Gets Early Relief with Marquette Date," *The Birmingham News*, March 13, 2006, p. 1-C.
62	If I sat up here . . . unfair to our guys.: Kirk, "Dead Just a Month Ago."
63	It's the first time I've cried . . . just went to Texas A&M.": Gold, p. 197.
63	"He was coming not . . . Bryant's retirement in 1982.: Gold, p. 195.
63	I cried because I'm so proud . . . I'm upset about losing him.: Gold, p. 197.
64	a self-admitted "bad kid": Scott, p. 166.
64	"had a lot of physical . . . a spiritual basis in his life.": Scott, p. 166.
64	"dysfunctional. I had a mom . . . victim of their environment.": Scott, p. 166.
64	Before he was out of junior . . . what I had learned at home,": Scott, p. 166.
64	he attended a revival . . . relationship with Jesus Christ.": Scott, pp. 166-67.
65	"the best game I've ever witnessed.": Ron Ingram, "4 OT's!" *The Birmingham News*, March 19, 1995, p. 01-B.
65	who re-entered the game . . . drop through the rim.: Ingram, "4 OT's!"
65	"I've never been involved . . . one of this length.: Ingram, "4 OT's!"
66	Sally Stabler was cold . . . 45 minutes before kickoff.": John Underwood, "Surge by the Tide," *Sports Illustrated*, Oct. 24,1966, http://sportsillustrated.cnn.com/vault/article/magazine/MAG1079177/index.htm, Feb. 22, 2010.
66	"nobody among the . . . bumping umbrellas [was] budging.": Underwood.
66	the snap was low . . . or two inside the left upright.": Underwood.
67	Two blocked kicks, three . . . and an inflatable Elvis.: Doug Segrest, "Bama Bowls Over Buckeyes," *The Birmingham News*, Jan. 3, 1995, p. 01-01.
67	with sluggish play, penalties, . . . burning love was deflated.: Segrest, "Bama Bowls Over Buckeyes."

67 A good team finds . . . what Alabama did.: Segrest, "Bama Bowls Over Buckeyes."

68 Bear Bryant said was the finest he ever coached: Scott, p. 121.

68 Before Musso's sophomore season, . . . Unleash the Italian Stallion.": Scott, p. 121.

68 Musso later played Canadian . . . been the inspiration.: Scott, pp. 121-22.

68 The nickname really embarrassed me for a long time.: Scott, p. 121.

69 "the unofficial longest field goal in college history.": Bolton, *The Basketball Tide*, p. 97.

69 As the first half was . . . as the half ended.: Bolton, *The Basketball Tide*, p. 97.

69 "When it went in . . . SEC games at home.: Bolton, *The Basketball Tide*, p. 99.

70 "If we're going to win . . . whip their offensive line.": Austin Murphy, "The Tide Is Turning," *Sports Illustrated*, Sept. 8, 2008, http://sportsillustrated.cnn.com/vault/article/magazine/MAG1144910/index.htm, Feb. 18, 2010.

70 "We got whipped about every way you can get whipped,": Murphy, "The Tide Is Turning."

70 "Doesn't matter how good . . . no hole to go through,": Murphy, "The Tide Is Turning."

70 I think God made it simple. Just accept Him and believe.: Bettinger, p. 47.

71 "Hutson is credited with inventing modern pass receiving": Gold, p. 62.

71 He forever changed the way. . . used the forward pass.: Gold, p. 53.

71 Coach Frank Thomas called him "the best player I ever coached.": Gold, p. 55.

71 when halfback Dixie Howell . . . against his coach's wishes,: Gold, p. 59.

72 Alabama and Ole Miss were ready . . . "the suits at ABC were nervous": Doug Segrest, "The Night the Tide Put College Ball on TV," *The Birmingham News*, Oct. 9, 2009, p. 1-C.

72 He set NCAA records . . . setting an Alabama standard: Segrest, "The Night the Tide."

72 Ole Miss blitzed . . . a tackle and scored.": Segrest, "The Night the Tide."

72 It became an iconic game . . . prime-time entertainment.: Segrest, "The Night the Tide."

73 Thompson evacuated his . . . while he was away.: Ray Melick, "Thompson to Fine-Tune His Game," *The Birmingham News*, Sept. 2, 2007, p. 15-C.

73 Thompson and his roommate . . . process all over again.: Melick, "Thompson to Fine-Tune His Game."

73 "It's been a wild ride,": Melick, "Thompson to Fine-Tune His Game."

73 It's just a blessing that it worked out this way for me.: Melick, "Thompson to Fine-Tune His Game."

74 In September 1995, Jackson . . . that his turn would come.: Doug Segrest, "Jackson Was Gone," *The Birmingham News*, Sept. 17, 1996, p. 01-C.

74 Darrell Blackburn, who led . . . a degenerative kidney.: Segrest, "Jackson Was Gone."

74 I don't think he . . . live without him.: Segrest, "Jackson Was Gone."

75 In 1961 it became official. Bear Bryant was a prophet.": Gold, p. 99.

75 He was present when . . . we would be national champions.": Gold, p. 99.

75 "I thought he was crazy.": Scott, p. 82.

75 after which an excited . . . because of the win.: Gold, p. 102.

75 You can't look at a rabbit and see how fast he can run.": Gold, p. 101.

76 "the greatest end in Alabama . . . since Joe Namath.": Scott, p. 132.

76 He didn't go out for . . . "The story begins": Scott, p. 132.

76 All is knew is that . . . I would catch it.: Scott, p. 132.

77 "the heart and soul" . . . have a monster game now.": Steve Irvine, "Bigger Than Shoes," *The Birmingham News*, March 25, 2004, p. 1-B.

78 Don't go! Don't go in there!": Ward, p. 136.

78 some Tide players prayed that Bear Bryant would not be hired.: Ward, p. 135.

78 "The one we didn't want . . . was, man, he's tough.": Ward, p. 136.

78 the initial workout in the . . . "It was brutal.": Ward, p. 136.

78 he quit every day . . . without moving -- totally exhausted.": Ward, p. 136.

78 I just wanted to live through [the] day.: Ward, p. 137.

79 "You have to pick your medicine. . . . execute other aspects.": Jones, "Run for the Roses," p. 61.

79 Coach Nick Saban decided . . . touchdown catch of his career.: Jones, "Run for the Roses," p. 61.

79 Put me in! . . . wide open in the end zone.: Jones, "Run for the Roses," p. 61.

80 "Traveling with the Snake . . . on the road with a rock star.": Gold, p. 129.

80 "I played fifteen years . . . it was real, real windy.": Gold, p. 135-36.

80 "I just went straight for that chain-link fence!": Gold, p. 136.

80 If the Bear came in person . . . some change in his pocket.: Gold, p. 130.

81 Dee decided to pull his starters, . . . This one is theirs.": Bolton, *The Basketball Tide*, p. 107.

82 "Gee, Coach, they don't . . . the last two years,": Pat Putnam, "Pride in the Red Jersey," *Sports Illustrated*, Oct. 11, 1971, http://sportsillustrated.cnn.com/vault/article/magazine/MAG1085387/index.htm, Feb. 22, 2010.

83 The squad had never had . . . sound of hammers and saws.: Steve Kirk, "Tide Pride Showing in World Series Debut," *The Birmingham News*, May 25, 2000, p. 01-D.

83 When first-team All-SEC . . . "This weekend.": Kirk, "Tide Pride Showing."

83 "The reporters in Arizona couldn't believe it,": Kirk, "Tide Pride Showing."

83 "despicable, vile, unprincipled scoundrels." MacArthur, p. 152.

83 [Playing in the World Series . . . such a short amount of time.: "Tide Earns First Ever Series Spot," *The Birmingham News*, May 22, 2000, p. 01-C.

84 reading the newspaper when . . . in the Sugar Bowl.: Hicks, p. 36.

84 "I thought Jack was going . . . where I had been.": Hicks, p. 36.

84 He enjoyed playing cornerback . . . anxious about playing defensive back.: Hicks, p. 38.

84 which overlooked naming . . . and put someone in.: Hicks, pp. 38-39.

84 I just know it caught me by surprise.: Hicks, p. 36.

85 with only 1:53 left in the . . . into a warm dressing room: Steve Kirk, "Plan to Kill Clock Turned into Key Tide Touchdown," *The Birmingham News*, Nov. 17, 2002, p. 10-B.

85 Coach Dennis Franchione and . . . 22 seconds left.: Kirk, "Plan to Kill."

85 by running the option . . . again and scored.: Kirk, "Plan to Kill."

85 Les Koenning and I just talked about getting a first down.: Kirk, "Plan to Kill."

86 The race for berths . . . a rise to fourth place.: Ian R. Rapoport, "2nd Ninth-Inning Comeback in 3 Days," *The Birmingham News*, 12 May 2008, p. 1-C.

86 "I was questioning, 'Why?'": Rapoport, "2nd Ninth-Inning Comeback."

86 he knew that the Florida . . . for Sunday afternoon games.: Rapoport, "2nd Ninth-Inning Comeback."

86   the most important win of the season.: Rapoport, "2nd Ninth-Inning Come-back."

86   With that situation -- curfew, two outs -- make him throw you out.: Rapoport, "2nd Ninth-Inning Comeback."

87   she inspired a little larceny . . . otherwise honest young man": Scott, p. 94.

87   "the finest player I ever coached" . . . the world has ever seen.": Scott, p. 93.

87   "I grew up picking cotton . . . like a day off.": Scott, p. 93.

87   The Jordan family farm raised . . . flour, salt, and pepper,": Scott, p. 94.

87   "I went home with Lee Roy . . . still got real upset over it.": Scott, p. 94.

88   "Every man played a . . . most of the time.": Bolton, *The Basketball Tide*, pp. 50-51.

88   "a large number of students . . . name of the University of Alabama.": Bolton, *The Basketball Tide*, p. 49.

88   "Not content with 'booing' . . . attempting to shoot fouls.": Bolton, *The Basketball Tide*, p. 49.

88   the opponents "are the guests . . . a most despicable practice.": Bolton, *The Basketball Tide*, pp. 49-50.

89   "It wasn't going to . . . We had a hunger.": Bill Bryant, "After Stewing for a Year, Tide Gets Revenge," *The Huntsville Times*, Dec. 6, 2009, http://www.al.com/sports/huntsvilletimes/bbryant.ssf?.base/sports, Dec. 9, 2009.

89   "Everybody was talking about . . . today it was McElroy.": Bryant.

89   Everything we did . . . to beat [Florida].: Jones, "Run for the Roses," p. 64.

90   "the defining hour of his youth.": Lars Anderson, "The 'Bama Defense," *Sports Illustrated*, July 13, 2009, http://sportsillustrated.ccn.com/vault/article/magazine/MAG1157675/index.htm, Feb. 18, 2010.

90   "the biggest tackle of the Bear Bryant era at Alabama.": Anderson, "The 'Bama Defense."

90   called the play that sent . . . to stop a run.: Anderson, "The 'Bama Defense."

90   defense coordinator Ken Donahue . . . State on third down.: Anderson, "The 'Bama Defense."

90   "face mask to face mask.": Anderson, "The Bama Defense."

90   "I actually broke my helmet, . . . everything out of me." Scott, p. 146.

90   To think I made an impact . . . it's just fantastic.: Scott, p. 143.

91   his "startling athleticism for a man his size": Lars Anderson, "Barrett Jones Leaving a Lasting Legacy at Alabama," *SI.com*, Jan. 1, 2013. http://sports illustrated.cnn.com/college-football-news/20130101/barrett-jones.

91   "most versatile offensive lineman in Crimson Tide history.": Anderson, "Barrett Jones Leaving a Lasting Legacy at Alabama."

91   "I may not be the biggest or fastest guy out there.": Anderson, "Barrett Jones Leaving a Lasting Legacy at Alabama."

91   He started playing the . . . been there all night,": Anderson, "Barrett Jones Leaving a Lasting Legacy at Alabama."

91   Barrett [Jones] is not only the . . . he's also probably the toughest.: Anderson, "Barrett Jones Leaving a Lasting Legacy at Alabama."

92   "You're never too old until you think you are.: Warner, p. 12.

92   Coaching is a young man's game.": Scott, p. 22.

92   he could no longer . . . while they were playing.: Scott, p. 22.

92   "There comes a time . . . that time has come.": Scott, p. 24.

92   Since 1979, he had suffered . . . he was pronounced dead.: Scott, p. 24.

92   Retire? I'd probably croak in a week.: Warner, p. 34.

CRIMSON TIDE

BIBLIOGRAPHY

Anderson, Lars. "Barrett Jones Leaving a Lasting Legacy at Alabama." *SI.com*. 1 Jan. 2013. http://sportsillustrated.cnn.com/college-football/news/20130101/barrett-jones.

-----. "The 'Bama Defense." *Sports Illustrated*. 13 July 2009. http://sportsillustrated.cnn.com/vault/article/magazine/MAG1157675/index.htm.

Atcheson, Wayne. *Faith of the Crimson Tide*. Grand Island, NE: Cross Training Publishing, 2000.

"Bear Bryant Knew How to Be Nice." *Redelephants*. http://www.redelephants.com/CoachBearBryant.html.

Beech, Mark. "The Tide Has Turned." *Sports Illustrated*. 10 Oct. 2005. http://sportsillustrated.cnn.com/vault/article/magazine/MAG1103865/index.htm.

Bettinger, Jim & Julie S. *The Book of Bowden*. Nashville: TowleHouse Publishers, 2001.

"Blind Golfer 'Reads' the Greens." *The Palm Beach Post*. 1 March 1971. http://news.google.com/newspapers?nid=1964&dat=19710301.

Bolton, Clyde. *The Basketball Tide: A Story of Alabama Basketball*. Huntsville: The Strode Publishers, 1977.

---. *The Crimson Tide: A Story of Alabama Football*. Huntsville: The Strode Publishers, 1972.

Browning, Al. *Third Saturday in October: The Game-by-Game Story of the South's Most Intense Football Rivalry*. Nashville: Cumberland House Publishing, Inc., 2001.

Bryant, Bill. "After Stewing for a Year, Tide Gets Revenge." *The Huntsville Times*. 6 Dec. 2009. http://www.al.com/sports/huntsvilletimes/bbryant.ssf?/base/sports.

"Charles A. Boswell." *Encyclopedia of Alabama*. http://www.encyclopediaofalabama.org/face/Article.jsp?id=h-1771.

Deford, Frank. "'I Do Love the Football.'" *Sports Illustrated*. 23 Nov. 1981. http://sportsillustrated.cnn.com/vault/article/magazine/MAG1125024/index.htm.

Estes, Gentry. "Hope Is Alive: Lunceford's Grand Slam Helps Alabama Avoid Elimination with Second Win of Day." *The Mobile Press-Register*. 31 May 2009. http://www.al.com/alabamabaseball/mobileregister/women.ssf?base/sports.

---. "Tuscaloosa Native Chris Smelley to Transfer Schools and Sports." *The Mobile Press-Register*. 9 Jan. 2009. http://blog.al.com/bamabeat/2009/01/alabama_could_soon_be_adding.html.

Glier, Ray. "Now Calling Pitches, Not Signals." *The New York Times*. 4 March 2009. http://www.nytimes.com/2009/03/05/sports/baseball/05smelley.html.

Gold, Eli. *Crimson Nation*. Nashville: Rutledge Hill Press, 2005.

Heim, Mark. "Alabama Baseball Coach Jim Wells Retires after 15 Years; Mitch Gaspard to Take Over." *The Mobile Press-Register*. 2 Sept. 2009. http://blog.al.com/press-register-sports/2009/09/alabama_baseball_coach_jim_wel.html.

Heller, Dick. "Refs Didn't Cotton to Off-Bench Stop." *The Washington Times*. 1 Jan. 2007. http://www.ricefootball.net/collegeinnwtstory.htm.

Hicks, Tommy. *Game of My Life: Alabama: Memorable Stories of Crimson Tide Football*. Champaign, IL: Sports Publishing L.L.C., 2006.

Holiday, Pete. "On the Mark: 'Bama Wins Championships and Now Heismans." *Yea Alabama 2009*. Hanover, MA: Maple Street Press LLC, 2010. 71-76.

Ingram, Ron. "4 OT's! Records Fall as Tide Women Win." *The Birmingham News*. 19 March 1995. 01-B.

Irvine, Steve. "Bigger Than Shoes: Pettway Drives Tide to Success in Any Footwear." *The Birmingham News*. 25 March 2004. 1-B.

---. "Laird Low-Key about SEC Record." *The Birmingham News*. 19 Feb. 2002. 6-C.

---. "One Is Done: Tide Knocks Off No. 1-Ranked Stanford to Advance to Sweet 16." *The Birmingham News*. 21 March 2004. 1-C.

---. "Rocky Stopped: Tide Ends Seven Years of Losing to Volunteers." *The Birmingham News*. 27 Oct. 2002. 1-B.

"Joe Namath." *Wikipedia, the free encyclopedia*. http://en.wikipedia.org/wiki/Joe_Namath.

Jones, Todd. "Run for the Roses: Alabama's Road to the BCS National Championship." *Yea Alabama 2009*. Hanover, MA: Maple Street Press LLC, 2010. 17-69.

---. "Title Wave: Alabama Rides Ingram, Defense to Break Championship Drought." *Yea Alabama 2009*. Hanover, MA: Maple Street Press LLC, 2010. 4-16.

Kennedy, Ray. "Battle for Braggin' Rights." *Sports Illustrated*. 9 Dec. 1974. http://sportsillustrated.cnn.com/vault/article/magazine/MAG1089323/index.htm.

Kirk, Steve. "Dead Just a Month Ago, Tide Revives." *The Birmingham News*. 11 Feb. 2006. 6-B.

---. "Not Like They Drew It Up: With a Draw Called, Tide's Decisive TD Comes When Hall Is Left Uncovered." *The Birmingham News*. 25 Sept. 2005. 1-C.

---. "Plan to Kill Clock Turned into Key Tide Touchdown." *The Birmingham News*. 17 Nov. 2002. 10-B.

---. "Tide Coach Embraces Slap-Hitting Speedster: Hug Convinces Rogers She Belonged on Team." *The Birmingham News*. 10 May 2006. 1-C.

---. "Tide Gets Early Relief with Marquette Date." *The Birmingham News*. 13 March 2006. 1-C.

---. "Tide Pride Showing in World Series Debut." *The Birmingham News*. 25 May 2000. 01-D.

Kirkpatrick, Curry. "Solution to a Thorny Problem." *Sports Illustrated*. 15 March 1982. http://sportsillustrated.cnn.com/vault/article/magazine/MAG1125307/index.htm.

Kirshenbaum, Jerry. "High Tide Washes over Vols." *Sports Illustrated*. 13 eb. 1978. http://sportsillustrated.cnn.com/vault/article/magazine/MAG1093316/index.htm.

Lake, Thomas. "The Shot That Saved Lives." *Sports Illustrated*. 16 March 2009.

CRIMSON TIDE

http://sportsillustrated.cnn.com/vault/article/magazine/MAG1153064/index.htm.

MacArthur, John. *Twelve Ordinary Men*. Nashville: W Publishing Group, 2002.

Melick, Ray. "A Serious Miler: Tide's Stephen Bolt Was First Alabamian to Run Sub-Four-Minute Mile and a Sub-2:15 Marathon." *The Birminghan News*. 28 May 2009. 1-C.

---. "Thompson to Fine-Tune His Game: Amateur Runner-Up Grooming for Pros." *The Birmingham News*. 2 Sept. 2007. 15-C.

Murphy, Austin. "The Tide Is Turning." *Sports Illustrated*. 8 Sept. 2008. http://sportsillustrated.cnn.com/vault/article/magazine/MAG1144910/index.htm.

---. "A Tidy Finish." *Sports Illustrated*. 14 Dec. 1992. http://sportsillustrated.cnn.com/vault/article/magazine/MAG1004647/index.htm.

"Pat Trammell." *Wikipedia, the free encyclopedia*. http://en.wikipedia.org/wiki/Pat_Trammell.

Putnam, Pat. "Pride in the Red Jersey." *Sports Illustrated*. 11 Oct. 1971. http://sportsillustrated.cnn.com/vault/article/magazine/MAG1085387/index.htm.

Rapoport, Ian R. "2nd Ninth-Inning Comeback in 3 Days: Tide Now Tied for 4th in SEC." *The Birmingham News*. 12 May 2008. 1-C.

---. "Apologetic Wells Returns as Coach: Says He Rushed Decision to Retire." *The Birmingham News*. 28 June 2007. 1-B.

---. "Smelley in On-Deck Circle for Tide: Ex-Gamecock Likely to Sit Out This Season." *The Birmingham News*. 18 Feb. 2009. 3-C.

---. "Turning Points: Changes Started During Practices for Bowl Game." *The Birmingham News*. 2 Dec. 2008. 1-c.

Rhoden, William C. "Dareus's Big Plays Surprised Even Him." *The New York Times*. 8 Jan. 2010. http://www.nytimes.com/2010/01/09/sports/ncaa football/09rhoden.html.

Scott, Richard. *Legends of Alabama Football*. Champaign, IL: Sports Publishing L.LC., 2004.

Segrest, Doug. "Bama Bowls Over Buckeyes: Late Rally in Citrus Cap [*sic*] 12-1 Season." *The Birmingham News*. 3 Jan. 1995. 01-01.

---. "Bama Mac-Dominates Penn: McDyess Sparks Tide's Overtime Win." *The Birmingham News*. 17 March 1995. 01-B.

---. "Bama Sacks Michigan to Send Stallings Home a Winner." *The Birmingham News*. 2 Jan. 1997. 01-C.

---. "Beatdown in T-Town: Tide Seniors Finally Get First Win over Auburn." *The Birmingham News*. 30 Nov. 2008. 3-C.

---. "Jackson Was Gone, But a Friend Brought Him Back to Bama." *The Birmingham News*. 17 Sept. 1996. 01-C.

---. "The Night the Tide Put College Ball on TV: Thrilling Win over Ole Miss Changed U.S. Viewing Habits." *The Birmingham News*. 9 Oct. 2009. 1-C.

---. "Raising the Bar: Patterson Lifts Bama Gymnastics to the Top and Lands in the ASHOF." *The Birmingham News*. 5 March 2003. 1-D.

---. "Success Came Early for UA Duo: Johnson, Watkins Shine for Final Four-Bound Tide." *The Birmingham News*. 30 March 1994. 1-01.

---. "Tiger, Tider HOF Bound: Tide's Lowe Played on 3 SEC Title Clubs." *The Birmingham News*. 1 May 2009. 3-B.

---. "Wells, Gaspard Would Make Good Team." *The Birmingham News*. 28 June 2007. 1-B.

---. "Wells Retires after 13 Seasons." *The Birmingham News*. 22 June 2007. 1-D.

Staples, Andy. "Ingram Won Heisman, But LB McClain Is Heart and Soul of Tide." *SI.com*. 5 Jan. 2010. http://sportsillustrated.cnn.com/2010/writers/andy_staples/01/04/rolando-mcclain/index.htm.

"Tide Earns First Ever Series Spot." *The Birmingham News*. 22 May 2000. 01-C.

Underwood. John. "Surge by the Tide." *Sports Illustrated*. 24 Oct. 1966. http://sportsillustrated.cnn.com/vault/article/magazine/MAG1079177/index.htm.

Wade, Don. *Always Alabama: A History of Crimson Tide Football*. New York: Simon & Schuster, 2006.

Wahl, Grant. "Playing Through the Pain." *Sports Illustrated*. 29 Jan. 2007. http://sportsillustrated.cnn.com/vault/article/magazine/MAG1104375/index.htm.

Warner, Chris, ed. *SEC Sports Quotes*. Baton Rouge: CEW Enterprises, 2002.

Wojciechowski, Gene. "Tide at Pinnacle of College Football." *ESPN.com*. 7 Jan. 2013. http://espn.go.com/college-football/bowls.

INDEX
(LAST NAME, DEVOTION DAY NUMBER)